D0305908

Lincoln College

1072317

# The Story of the Piano

# The Story of the Piano

*Kenneth van Barthold and*
*David Buckton*

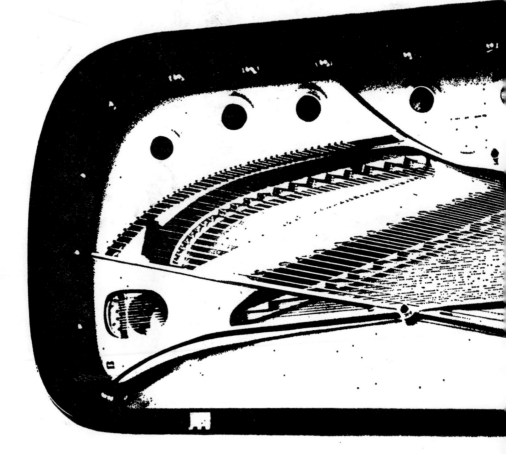

*British Broadcasting Corporation*

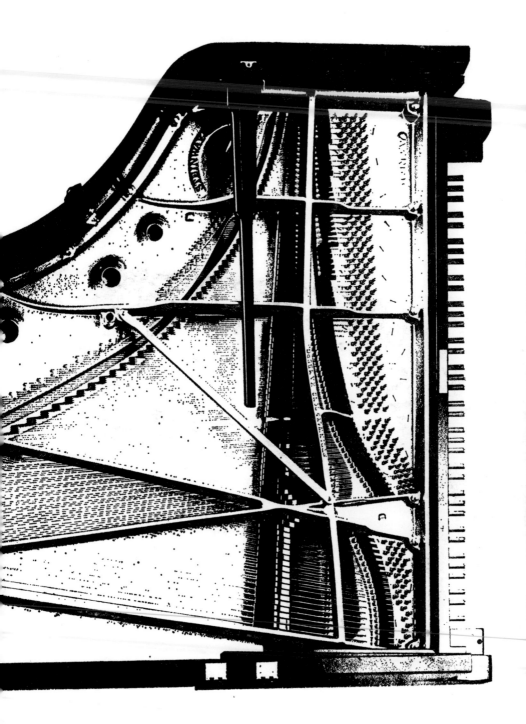

Published by the
British Broadcasting Corporation
35 Marylebone High Street
London W1M 4AA

ISBN 0 563 12580 2

© Kenneth van Barthold and David Buckton 1975
First published 1975

NOTTINGHAMSHIRE

5312187

COUNTY LIBRARY

Printed in Scotland by
T. & A. Constable Ltd, Edinburgh

# *Contents*

Preface   7

1   A Familiar Instrument with a Familiar Sound?   11

2   Before the Piano   17

3   Cristofori – Inventor of the Piano   25

4   England   35

5   Vienna   49

6   Paris   59

7   The Domestic Piano   67

8   Oddities   83

9   The Modern Piano   91

Appendices   105

The diagrams of piano actions in this book are designed to show the non-specialist how these actions work. For this purpose they are given in the form of simplified adaptations and should not be taken as accurate representations of specific pianos. Anyone wishing to study more complete diagrams should refer to technical books on the subject.

*Acknowledgment is due to the following for permission to reproduce illustrations:*

page 15, Mary Evans Picture Library; facing 16, (top) Victoria and Albert Museum, London, (bottom) The Russell Collection of Harpsichords, University of Edinburgh; facing 17, (top) Deutsches Museum, München, (bottom) Musikinstrumenten Museum, Karl-Marx-Universität, Leipzig; 23, Mary Evans Picture Library; facing 32, (bottom) David Buckton; facing 33, (top) The Russell Collection of Harpsichords (in the possession of the Duke of Wellington), (bottom) Colt Clavier Collection (photograph by Michael Freeman); facing 48, (top) George Balfour, (bottom) Colt Clavier Collection (Freeman); facing 49 (top & bottom), facing 64 (top & bottom), Colt Clavier (Freeman); between 64 & 65, (top left) Germanisches Nationalmuseum, Nürnberg, (top right) Radio Times Hulton Picture Library, (bottom left & right) Colt Clavier (Freeman); facing 65, (top) Radio Times Hulton Picture Library, (bottom) Colt Clavier (Freeman); facing 80, (top) Radio Times Hulton Picture Library, (bottom) Colt Clavier (Freeman); facing 81, (top) Colt Clavier (Freeman), (bottom) The British Piano Museum; 82, Mansell Collection; facing 88 (top & bottom), Colt Clavier (Freeman); between 88 & 89, (top left) Smithsonian Institution, photo no. 56445A, (bottom left) Steinway & Sons, New York, (right) Steinway (top & bottom right, photo Freeman); facing 89, (top & bottom) © Steinway factory (photo Freeman).

The diagrams were by Sue Ribbans from originals by David Buckton.

# Preface

In August 1970, at a 'fringe' concert of the Edinburgh Festival, I heard Richard Burnett play his Conrad Graf Viennese piano, which is very similar to the Graf piano owned by Beethoven for the last three years of his life. After the concert he let me run my fingers over it. That started it all.

Seventeen years ago I started studying and performing from facsimile and Urtext (that is 'original' text) editions, and have been slowly evolving a style of interpretation which seems valid, at least to me. After meeting Dick Burnett I began to have access to the original instruments too, for he and Derek Adlam have a fine collection of them at Finchcocks in Kent. A few weeks of playing these instruments clinched all, or very nearly all, my slowly evolving ideas about style. The previous seventeen years hadn't been wasted. My debt to Dick Burnett is incalculable.

It occurred to me that these early pianos would make a fascinating subject for a film. So I approached David Buckton; his enthusiasm was immediate and the project was soon in hand. Making 'How did it sound to Beethoven – the story of piano sound through 250 years' took eighteen months, a lot of patience and a great deal of travelling, since we had to go to the instruments rather than bring them to us. Now there is this book.

We would like at once to make two disclaimers. First, the book is *not* a comprehensive study of the piano. It tries to pick out the more important threads of the story and show how they contributed to the development of the piano's sound. As far as possible we have left excessive technical details out of the main part of the book. For those with a technical bent, there is an appendix on the principal types of piano action mentioned in the story. Second, although we reckon we now know quite a lot about the subject, we do not consider ourselves top experts on the mechanics of early pianos. We have met and picked the brains of people who really are experts and we are only too aware of the gaps in our knowledge. Nevertheless, the responsibility for what appears in this book is ours, and we can only ask to be forgiven for any mistakes.

We obviously referred to many sources but two of them proved indispensable: Rosamund Harding's book *History of the Piano-Forte*, which is encyclopaedic, and Arthur Loesser's *Men, Women and Pianos*, which is highly entertaining and puts the instrument firmly into its social and historical context.

Instrument-collectors, builders and restorers are a very special breed of enthusiasts. They have taken us into their confidence and in several cases became our friends. The Colt Clavier Collection, the private property of Mr C. F. Colt at Bethersden in Kent, was the starting-point and basis for our project. Mr Colt put it at our disposal and was unfailingly helpful. Derek Adlam, apart from his partnership with Dick Burnett, also used to help look after the instruments at the Colt Collection. I owe him special thanks for putting up with odd phone calls on technical matters and for urgently posting me replacement strings – they always seem to break just before some vital concert. I am a very great admirer of his craftsmanship, which I rate amongst the highest I have come across. He has a particular gift for restoring these old instruments so that they really *speak*.

We made shorter but none the less enjoyable visits to several other collections: the Russell Collection of Edinburgh University, administered by Dr Peter Williams and cared for by John Barnes, who was our consultant on technical matters throughout the film. I have known John for some years and he has played a great part in giving me any knowledge I may have acquired either about these instruments or the problems of playing them; the Victoria and Albert Museum, where Maurice Cochrane good-humouredly undertook the thankless task of bringing the instruments out of their glass cases and fighting against the clock to get them into the shape his very high standards demand; the Beethoven House in Bonn where we filmed amidst the hubbub of a Carnival Day and where Mike Savage, the BBC sound recordist, had his tie cut off, as is the custom, by a pretty German girl; and last, the Music Instrument Museum of the Karl Marx University at Leipzig which we finally reached after some hair-raising administrative entanglements with the East German authorities, and where Professor Petzoldt and his staff could not have been kinder or more helpful to us. It was an Aladdin's cave of musical instruments!

Two piano firms have been invaluable: Steinways in London, who put their factory at our disposal so that we could see and film their fine craftsmanship, and Broadwoods where Stewart Broadwood made all their records and correspondence available to us. The Piano Publicity Association have provided us with much useful information and statistics on recent piano manufacture in this country, and have made available their *Survey of Piano Ownership and Usage within Great Britain*.

Then finally there are our respective wives. Both have full careers – David's is a teacher and mine works in stained glass. They have seen many projects come and go. This one has particularly involved them, and their criticisms and advice have been most valuable.

KENNETH VAN BARTHOLD

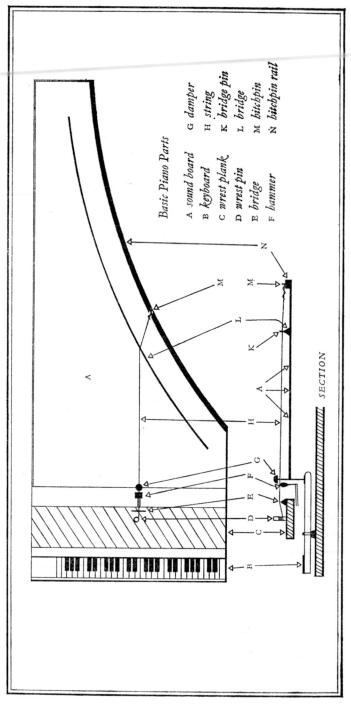

Basic Piano Parts

A sound board
B keyboard
C wrest plank
D wrest pin
E bridge
F hammer
G damper
H string
K bridge pin
L bridge
M hitchpin
N hitchpin rail

SECTION

# I

# A Familiar Instrument with a Familiar Sound?

If there is any one musical instrument people feel they know it is surely the piano. There it stands in millions of homes, part of the very furniture, lovingly dusted and adorned with those glamourised photographs of Mum when she was still in pigtails. For 200 years millions of children have spent agonising hours grappling with it; trying to co-ordinate mind and body so as to harness its eloquence. At school most of us have sung to it. It is *the* accompanying instrument. In its other role as a solo instrument it is pre-eminent. Its greatest exponents are household names and the war horses of its repertoire are known to millions of us all over the world.

As always happens with such familiar objects, they are taken for granted; they come to rest on a mountain of assumptions. Even among professional musicians, including pianists themselves, there are very few who understand the piano's construction or how it evolved. Yet even a minimal understanding of what happens between one's finger pressing down the key and the hammer striking the string increases one's control of the instrument.

Then there are those assumptions. For instance to most of us it seems perfectly natural that a note should go on sounding as long as we keep the key pressed down. Yet if the hammer were attached immovably to the key, pressing the key down would have the very opposite effect: it would keep the hammer pressed against the string and actually stop it from vibrating and continuing to sound. This, the fundamental problem of the piano action, took a long time to overcome and was solved in a variety of ways.

Another assumption is 'good tone'. We all know what that should be. If you have ever bought a piano you will easily recall that plush saleroom with all those gleaming pianos and the smooth salesman caressing his way through some suitably mushy bit of Chopin, having earlier that morning carefully polished up the golden letters of the magical name Steinway, Bechstein, Blüthner or whatever. Never mind the price, just listen to the beautiful tone! Of course we all know what good tone is. We adjust our stereo, if we are rich enough to possess one, until we get it. After hearing a piano recital few of us dare criticise the accuracy or the style of the performance, but we do feel free to comment on the quality of sound the pianist produced. After all that is something we really do know about.

Yet this is the most monstrous assumption of all. Our concept of good tone is completely different from Beethoven's or Mozart's. A radical change took place between about 1815 and 1850 and it is empty arrogance to assume that it was 'progress'. It is often said that Beethoven would have been thrilled by the sound of our great nine-foot Concert Grands: the probability is that he would have been most put out and upset by it.

But this is surmise. What is worth labouring is that it is our post-1850 concept of good tone that is the deviation. There is some kind of common denominator of timbre right through until that point, not just on the piano but in virtually all music. Let us put aside for the moment the last 300 years of Western European music. There still exist many instruments that pre-date that period. Let us examine a few.

There is the hurdy-gurdy; the bagpipes, or the

Indian snake charmer's pipe; the Indonesian Gamelan Orchestra, the Indian sitar, or the Japanese koto. These instruments fall into the usual categories of strings, wind and percussion. The first two categories are sustaining instruments, and different as the sound of the hurdy-gurdy may be from the bagpipes each has a nasal, reedy, slightly thin tone which relates it to the other. The gamelan orchestra, sitar and koto, plucked and percussive instruments, make a jangling, often tinsel-like, silvery sound. If left free to vibrate they again produce this nasal timbre. Anyone who has heard an Arab sing knows that the human voice can produce something very similar. There is a common denominator of sound here stretching across many centuries and the whole world. Those hearing it must have considered it 'good tone', and 'beautiful'.

In certain cases it is easy to relate this sound to some of the European instruments: the Hautboy – now our modern oboe – has a nasal sound; the guitar has the jangle. In other cases it can seem more difficult. The baroque flute or the viol family seem to make a smooth sound; yet compared with the modern flute and violin, which they father, they are thinner, more silvery, less rounded and mellifluous. The same applies to the baroque organ compared with the great nineteenth-century organs. The difference is there even if on occasion it is only relative. The modern sound is more oily.

This difference is crucial to the story of the piano, for its precursors, the clavichord and harpsichord, made the old 'mainstream' kind of sound, jangly, silvery, on occasion slightly nasal. And most important of all, *so did the early piano*, the so-called 'fortepiano'. It made a sound not unlike that of the harpsichord. Then around 1820 the sound began to change – not

13

just on the piano, but on most instruments. The whole concept of good tone changed.

This change, which must have been one of taste, was part of a wider, sometimes larger process. It can be seen in other things, for instance in the difference between the clothes of the eighteenth and nineteenth centuries: the brighter, clearer satins and silks of the former and the thicker, more sombre textiles of the latter. In the crisp elegant lines of eighteenth-century furniture as opposed to the more rounded shapes of their nineteenth-century equivalents. It occurred in the visual arts. The terracotta and gold colours of many late medieval church wall-decorations somehow match the nasal and jangling sound: the tone of the nineteenth-century piano matches those flowing rounded illustrations so common in Victorian books (remember those illustrated Shakespeares and Bibles).

The significance of all this is enormous. If the piano did not make a recognisably 'modern' sound until around 1850, by that time Mozart, Haydn, Beethoven, Schubert, Mendelssohn and Chopin were dead, and most of the better-known pieces by Schumann and Liszt had already been composed. Thus the core of the piano's repertoire was written for an instrument that sounded very different from ours and most music-lovers have no idea what it should sound like.

It was only in the nineteenth century that people began to play 'dead music', that is the music of preceding generations. Until then, if music was required, it was written for the occasion with little thought of the past or the future. We owe the second half of the nineteenth century a great deal for beginning to resuscitate the music of Bach, Handel, Mozart, Beethoven and countless others. But the nineteenth century believed in progress. It felt its instruments to be better than its predecessors' and used them unashamedly. It had applied the same process of improvement to the Gothic architectural masterpieces it so lovingly copied and restored. We are inclined to think differently. We have developed more historical consciousness. There is, after all, a precedent. When the harpsichord first reappeared in the 1920s many considered its sound unsympathetic, virtually unmusical. Now most of us accept it, many of us indeed prefer it, and it has completely changed our approach to the music of Bach, Scarlatti and Handel. Will the same soon happen to the music written for the fortepiano?

This book tells the story of the piano, from the first delicate instruments of around 1700 to the great powerful instruments of today – over 250 years of pianos and

*Roman Clavicembalo or Harpsichord. A.D. 1521.*

their sound. It tells how they were built and what their function in society was. But their sound it can only describe; and yet it is the sound of the early pianos that is the first thing that strikes one. It may take a big effort of adaptation to accept it, especially in the music of composers such as Beethoven and Mozart with which we are so familiar. But once accepted the results are little short of a revelation. If reading this book stimulates anyone to find out more about it, it will have fulfilled one of its functions. For the rest it may make you pause next time you are about to strum your favourite piece and cause you to reflect on the wonder of this extraordinary instrument and all the skill, inventiveness and affection that have gone into its development.

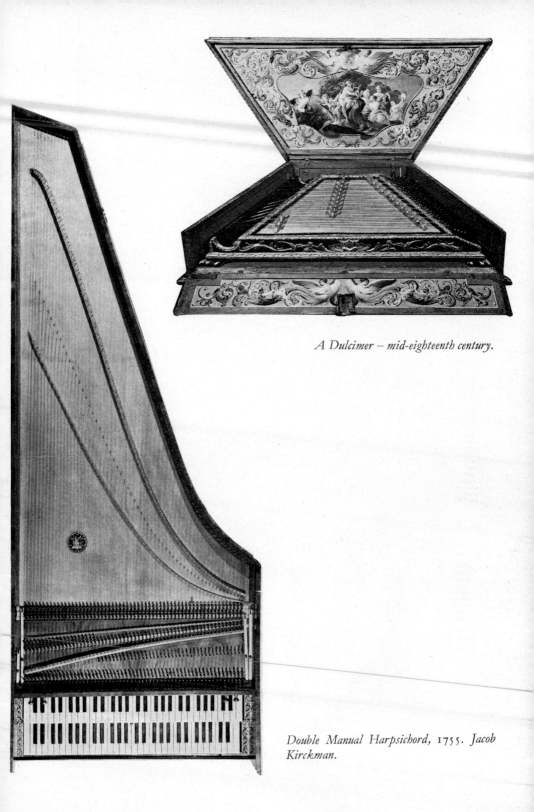

*A Dulcimer – mid-eighteenth century.*

*Double Manual Harpsichord,* 1755. *Jacob Kirckman.*

*Clavichord, 1702. Johan Weiss.*

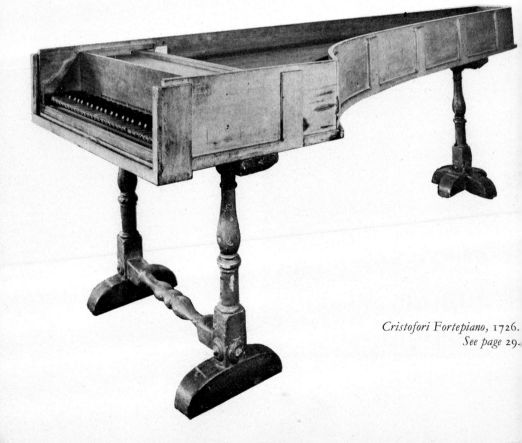

*Cristofori Fortepiano, 1726.*
*See page 29.*

# 2
## Before The Piano

To understand the arrival of the piano one must take into account the musical scene of the early 1700s when it first appeared. Its arrival must have been opportune indeed, for within 150 years it was to oust all its competitors and become and remain the most prevalent of all musical instruments. There were in the early 1700s three families of keyboard instruments: those where the sound was made by wind blown through pipes (the organ); those where it was made by plucking the string (the harpsichord family); and those where it was made by striking the string (the clavichord). The last two can properly be considered the fathers of the piano; being a wind instrument, the organ plays no part in this story.

The plucking instruments, the harpsichord and the virginals or spinet, were the most widely used keyboard instruments of the time. The name 'spinet' is an English corruption of the French word 'épinette', introduced into this country at the time of Charles II who, having spent many years exiled in France, brought back a host of gallicisms. Up to then this instrument had been called the virginals, presumably on account of its association with young ladies who were deemed its most suitable exponents. Domestically the harpsichord, or more frequently the spinet, was the mainstay of amateur music-making, even though its costliness reserved it for the few amongst the newly expanding bourgeoisie who could afford it. The harpsichord's main function was very similar to that of the piano in a modern jazz band. It was part of the rhythm section in nearly all ensemble music, where its characteristic jangle could help maintain the beat and its capacity to play chords could thicken out the harmonic texture. For these reasons it was also the most usual single accompanying instrument in, for instance, recitative. One might call these its public functions.

The word public should be used with care, for there were as yet no public paid-entry concerts as such. The Concerts Spirituels in Paris, amongst the earliest, were to begin in 1725. Instrumental music was the delight and privilege of the great aristocratic and royal households which had the means to employ full-time orchestras and composers for their exclusive entertainment. Some were even rich enough to afford the latest new-fangled craze from Italy – Opera. The recitative or story-telling parts of an opera were usually accompanied by just a harpsichord. This operatic technique of story-telling interspersed with arias or choruses (during which the dramatic action stood still) was soon adapted to religious music where it became the cantata and oratorio. Here again the harpsichord was used, both to accompany the recitatives and to fill out the orchestral texture in the remainder. It was a background instrument. It had a solo repertoire, but this was reserved largely for more informal or domestic occasions. That repertoire consisted of shortish pieces either in popular dance forms or descriptive of easily recognisable trivia such as the French composers specialised in – Daquin's *Cuckoo* is a well-known example. The harpsichord had as yet no function as a solo concerto instrument: its first use as such by J. S. Bach was a quarter of a century away. The idea of playing one instrument in public on its own for an hour in what we would now call a solo recital was as yet unheard of.

Harpsichords were to be found in the homes of most aristocrats, indeed the more opulent amongst them had whole collections of them, works of art in themselves, ornate and richly decorated. It was the keeper of one of these collections who was to invent the piano. For those who could not afford a harpsichord there was the spinet, a small simpler version of the harpsichord. The possession of one of these instruments was a definite social asset. It provided the excuse for musical evenings to which one could invite rich and influential people.

We must now pause to consider the basic principles of stringed keyboard instruments. They all consist of metal strings, stretched tight and set in vibration. Because strings vibrating on their own make hardly any noise, they are stretched over a wooden bridge which is glued to a soundboard. The soundboard is a sheet of fairly thin resonant wood whose function is to amplify the vibrations of the strings so that they can be heard as musical tones. The stretching of the strings has to be adjustable so as to produce the notes of the scale: the tighter the string the higher the note. So at one end each string is attached to a 'hitchpin' which secures it to the frame and at the other it is wound round a 'wrest pin' which can be turned round to tighten or loosen it.

The essential difference between different types of keyboard instrument is how the strings are set in vibration. In the harpsichord there is a long thin piece of wood, called the jack, which rises up beside each string and reaches down to the key beneath. Set in this jack is a small plectrum. When the key is pressed down it pushes up the jack in such a way that the plectrum plucks the string to make it sound. When the key is released the jack moves down and, by means of a little tongue set in it, the plectrum can slide back past the string without sounding it again. This mechanism is exactly the same in both spinet and harpsichord. What distinguishes the instruments are various other characteristics.

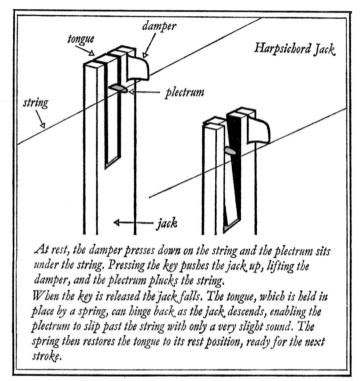

At rest, the damper presses down on the string and the plectrum sits under the string. Pressing the key pushes the jack up, lifting the damper, and the plectrum plucks the string.

When the key is released the jack falls. The tongue, which is held in place by a spring, can hinge back as the jack descends, enabling the plectrum to slip past the string with only a very slight sound. The spring then restores the tongue to its rest position, ready for the next stroke.

The spinet is the more modest. It has only one keyboard, and the strings are usually strung more or less parallel to the keyboard, unlike the harpsichord where they are at right angles. The harpsichord is more complex. The bigger ones had two keyboards, each with its own set of strings. By 1700 most of them were capable of some kind of change of registration. This is a term used to describe ways of varying the octave pitch or sound of any given note. For instance, by having a duplicate set of strings for each note, tuned an octave higher and plucked by a duplicate set of jacks which could be brought into play by pushing a lever, the player would immediately have three options open to him. First, the original set of jacks and strings on their own; second, the alternative set of jacks and strings which made each note sound an octave higher; and third, the two sets of jacks and strings working simultaneously making each key pressed down responsible for the sounding of two strings an octave apart (called 'coupling'). In addition many harpsichords carried an alternative set of jacks for each note with different plectra. If one set of plectra were made of quills the alternatives might be made of leather. This, of course, varies the texture of the sound.

The other predecessor of the piano was the clavichord. This instrument was particular to Germany, where it enjoyed an enormous popularity. It was essentially a domestic instrument, far simpler and consequently far cheaper to build than the spinet. It too had a set of strings parallel to the keyboard but they were sounded by a small piece of metal called the tangent set directly in the key. When the key was depressed the tangent struck the string and stayed in contact with it, producing the note. Being metal it could do this without stopping the strings from vibrating. This method of sounding the string also provided a bonus. The direct contact from the finger through the key and tangent to the string, the source of the sound, gave the player control of the volume of a note – the harder he hit it the louder it sounded. This control set the clavichord quite apart from any other kind of keyboard instrument of the time. The desire for this direct control was to play a large part in the future popularity of the piano. Meanwhile the clavichord had one great disadvantage. Its overall volume was so small that it was quite unusable as a major ensemble instrument. That role was the harpsichord's. But since the strings on a harpsichord were plucked, there was only a fleeting instant of contact with the string and virtually no control of either timbre or volume of sound.

The clavichord then was an ideal domestic instrument capable of fine gradation from note to note. We know that it was very popular in J. S. Bach's family. Its widespread use undoubtedly helped create a favourable climate for the arrival of the piano – whose survival in those early fragile years owes much to the Germans. It was they who took it over from the Italians, and were the first to develop it, write for it and play it. There is much nonsense talked about musical and unmusical nations. It would seem highly improbable that the incidence of inborn musical gift should stop and start this or that side of a frontier. But for musical talent to grow it needs the opportunity, and this is what the Germans seem to have been so much better at creating.

Fragmented into a rash of dukedoms and principalities, eighteenth-century Germany's aristocrats vied with each other to retain the finest musicians in their establishments. Although this happened to some extent in other European countries at the time, the sheer number of them in Germany was far greater. In addition, every German town of any size had its pool of musicians, retained and paid for by the town council to perform for civic or religious functions. The Lutheran church had changed the old forms of worship – church services had been democratised, and ordinary people took part and felt involved in what was happening. In musical terms it meant they joined in the singing of the chorales. The base of musical life was broad indeed. So there was a need for a simple, cheap but comprehensive domestic instrument for practice, performance and instruction. Keyboard instruments have always proved ideal for early musical instruction, providing as they do both an aural and visual dictionary of sounds. It is even probable that the very shape of our present-day keyboard resulted from a calibration of the octave used in the Middle Ages to help the monks learn their notes. The clavichord fulfilled most of these needs.

Yet as time passed the desire grew for an instrument capable of the power of the harpsichord and the finger-responsiveness of the clavichord. This desire was probably given impetus by the success of a Saxon called Pantaleon Hebenstreit in the very early 1700s. He built and played on a dulcimer of almost unbelievable pro-

W. Hollar inv.
1935

portions. The dulcimer, a very old instrument, consists of a soundboard with its strings – which are hit with sticks – strung across two bridges. Pantaleon's dulcimer was six feet long, four times the size of the normal one, and strung with about 200 strings of either metal or gut. He gave it the whole chromatic scale and with different coverings on his sticks could get a variety of tone colours and variations of loud and soft that must have created a sensation wherever he went. He played it to King Louis XIV at Versailles, to the Emperor in Vienna and at the Court of Saxony. It became widely known in the small musical circles of Europe. Its power, resonance and immediate responsiveness must have deeply impressed contemporary instrument-makers. Yet it had drawbacks, not least that it was extremely difficult to play – Hebenstreit himself seems to have been the only person really to master it. This could be overcome if its string-striking principle could be harnessed to a keyboard. It was this combination that resulted in the fortepiano – the 'loud soft' – the first comparatively powerful instrument with finger-control of the volume of its notes.

# 3
# Cristofori – Inventor of the Piano

In the year 1700 the great Italian violin-maker Antonio Stradivari, working in Cremona, was producing some of the finest violins of his Golden Period. The violin had already established its precedence over the viol family as a brighter instrument capable of a much wider range of expression. At the same time, in Naples some 500 miles to the south, the new Italian opera, with its emphasis on the solo aria, was flourishing in the hands of Alessandro Scarlatti. With the violin, and especially with the human voice, the individual was able to express himself in a very direct way, with the minimum barrier between himself and the actual sound. So it is perhaps not surprising that the attempts, which were being made in several parts of Europe, to make the harpsichord expressive should have met with their first real success in Italy.

The harpsichord, for all its limitations as an 'expressive' instrument, was very suitable for accompanying both voice and violin. It had a tone quality that people were used to and liked, and it could provide a firm foundation above which the solo performer could develop and embellish his melodies. But although Northern Italy had been the world centre of harpsichord-making in the sixteenth century, the Italians had never expended a lot of energy in developing the instrument beyond its accompanying role and that of filling out the harmonies. There is a very distinctive type of Italian harpsichord that is ideal for these purposes. It is light in construction, and has a bright tone that contrasts with the fuller, fruitier sound of the heavier harpsichords being made in Holland and Germany.

Bartolommeo Cristofori, who was born in Padua in 1655, was a maker of just this type of harpsichord. In 1700 he was in Florence, employed by Prince Ferdinand, son of Grand Duke Cosimo III, as his keeper of musical instruments. And he was working on the idea of a keyboard instrument that could produce a varied dynamic response directly by control of the fingers, as in the clavichord, but more powerful, so that the player could offer a greater range of expression in his performance. All the evidence suggests that it was Cristofori who made the first practical piano in about 1709.

Not too much is known of Cristofori's life, but we have direct evidence of his first piano, which was called a 'gravicembalo col piano e forte' (a keyboard instrument with soft and loud), because of the visit of the Marchese Scipione Maffei to Prince Ferdinand in 1709. Maffei was apparently trying to get the Prince's patronage for a new paper called *Giornale dei Letterati d'Italia*. He must have met Cristofori and seen his new invention, for he subsequently described it in some detail in his *Giornale* and even included a diagram showing how the action of the piano worked. Although this was probably drawn from memory and would perhaps be difficult to convert directly into a working piano action, the diagram does show that Cristofori had solved a basic problem of piano design.

First it has to be realised that the intention of the early piano experimenters was always to use something softer than metal to strike the strings, and in fact the chosen material was leather. But if a leather covered hammer were attached direct to the key, as is the metal tangent of the clavichord, then the action of pressing the key down would press the hammer against the

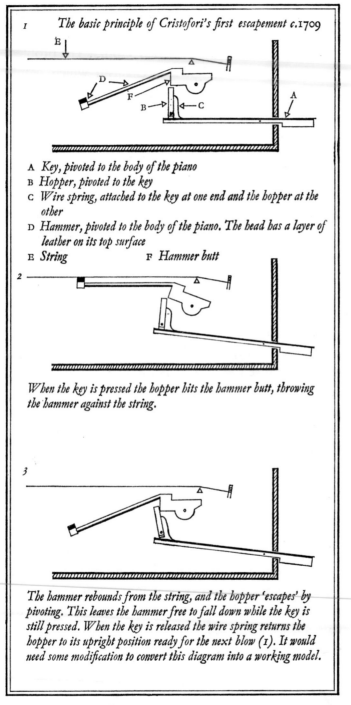

*1  The basic principle of Cristofori's first escapement c.1709*

A  *Key, pivoted to the body of the piano*
B  *Hopper, pivoted to the key*
C  *Wire spring, attached to the key at one end and the hopper at the other*
D  *Hammer, pivoted to the body of the piano. The head has a layer of leather on its top surface*
E  *String*  F  *Hammer butt*

*When the key is pressed the hopper hits the hammer butt, throwing the hammer against the string.*

*The hammer rebounds from the string, and the hopper 'escapes' by pivoting. This leaves the hammer free to fall down while the key is still pressed. When the key is released the wire spring returns the hopper to its upright position ready for the next blow (1). It would need some modification to convert this diagram into a working model.*

string and hold it there. Thus the hammer would start the string vibrating but immediately stop it, and we would be left with just a muffled 'clonk'. The problem therefore was to design a mechanism which would allow the single movement of the key being pressed down to result in two movements of the hammer, first to strike the string, and then to come away from it, leaving the string free to continue vibrating.

Cristofori's solution was what is known as the escapement, and its invention was crucial for the future development of the piano's expressive capacity. The escapement has since taken many different forms, but the principle of Cristofori's first successful design was that instead of the hammer being impelled directly by the key there is an intervening piece of wood, called a hopper, which is attached to the key by a pivot at its lower end. It is therefore the hopper that actually hits the hammer butt, and impels the hammer towards the string. Because the hopper is pivoted, it can then slip past the hammer butt, or 'escape' from it, so that the hammer is able to rebound from the string without being obstructed by the top of the hopper. In fact the hammer butt rests on the *side* of the hopper until the key is released, when everything falls back to its starting position and a little wire spring returns the hopper to its upright position.

In Cristofori's design there is another lever between the key and the hopper. This 'intermediate lever', as it is called, doesn't alter the principle described above, but changes the ratio of key movement to hammer movement. It also controls the movement of the damper, which falls away from the string when the key is pressed, and is pushed back up against the string when the key is released, thus stopping the string from continuing to sound.

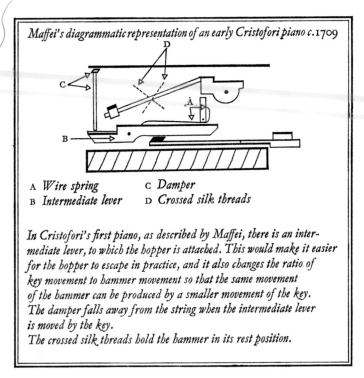

*Maffei's diagrammatic representation of an early Cristofori piano c.1709*

A *Wire spring*       c *Damper*
B *Intermediate lever*   D *Crossed silk threads*

*In Cristofori's first piano, as described by Maffei, there is an intermediate lever, to which the hopper is attached. This would make it easier for the hopper to escape in practice, and it also changes the ratio of key movement to hammer movement so that the same movement of the hammer can be produced by a smaller movement of the key. The damper falls away from the string when the intermediate lever is moved by the key.*
*The crossed silk threads hold the hammer in its rest position.*

There are no known examples of this first model by Cristofori, but three of his later pianos survive. One, made in 1726, is kept in the Music Instrument Museum in the Karl Marx University of Leipzig. It is completely original apart from the necessary replacement of one or two small parts and strings, and is in very good playing order.

We should now consider what sort of instrument this is, and for comparison we need to look not to the modern piano but to the harpsichord. First its shape is just that of a single-manual Italian harpsichord, and indeed Cristofori made a harpsichord in the same year which to outward appearances is virtually identical. This instrument too is in the Leipzig Museum. The fortepiano[1] appears very small and its range is only four

[1] The word 'fortepiano' has no technical validity but is often used for convenience to describe the early wood framed instruments with leather hammers.

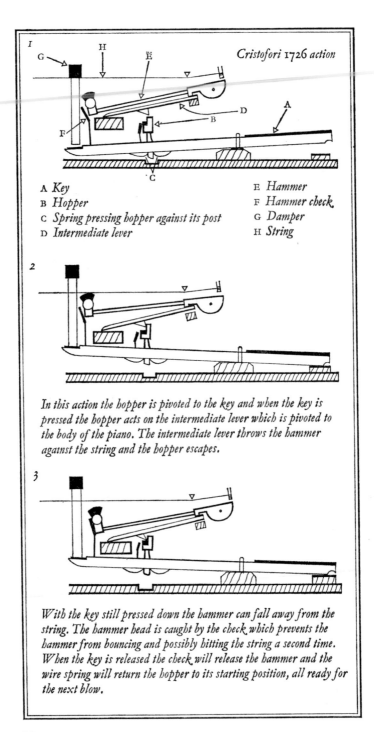

1

*Cristofori* 1726 *action*

A *Key*
B *Hopper*
C *Spring pressing hopper against its post*
D *Intermediate lever*
E *Hammer*
F *Hammer check*
G *Damper*
H *String*

2

*In this action the hopper is pivoted to the key and when the key is pressed the hopper acts on the intermediate lever which is pivoted to the body of the piano. The intermediate lever throws the hammer against the string and the hopper escapes.*

3

*With the key still pressed down the hammer can fall away from the string. The hammer head is caught by the check which prevents the hammer from bouncing and possibly hitting the string a second time. When the key is released the check will release the hammer and the wire spring will return the hopper to its starting position, all ready for the next blow.*

octaves – two octaves each side of middle C – which is not much more than half the range of a modern Grand. It has the same light construction and square tail as the comparable harpsichord, and the same thin strings, two to each note, but now each pair of strings, instead of being plucked by plectra set in jacks, is struck by a hammer. The hammer itself is very small and light, and consists of a shank made of Italian cedar and, at the striking end, a cylinder of strong paper with a little leather pad glued to the upper surface. It is this leather pad which actually strikes the strings. There are no foot pedals, and no means at all of sustaining a note after the finger has left the key (the misnamed 'loud' pedal of later pianos). There is, however, the equivalent of the 'soft' pedal – the *una corda* (one string). For this the keyboard and action are slid sideways so that the hammers strike only one out of each pair of strings, thereby producing a quieter sound. The keyboard has to be physically moved by hand, so that the *una corda* effect can only be produced when there is a hand free to do it.

The action of this piano is already much more advanced than Cristofori's first designs, and it incorporates a hammer check of a sort that is in use right up to the present day. The purpose of this check is to catch the hammer when it rebounds from the string, and prevent it from bouncing and possibly hitting the string a second time. The hammer is held in this way until the key is released when it falls back to its rest position.

What then is the sound of this instrument? Sound is difficult to describe, but this fortepiano has none of the full, rounded, smooth quality of the present-day piano. But nor does it have the brittle bright attack of the plucked harpsichord. In a way it's a mixture of these two sounds – still light and delicate, as determined by its thin strings and light wood frame, but with the sharpness softened by the relatively soft leather pad of the hammer. Most important of all, it has a remarkable and effective dynamic range, nowhere near the power of the modern piano but still far more than the clavichord was able to offer.

This capacity for variation between loud and soft would have been quite obvious to the first owner of such a fortepiano. What was not so obvious was that the instrument needed to be played in a quite different way. People were slow to realise that it was not just *overall* loudness and softness that had been made possible, but the *relative* loudness of individual notes in a phrase, and even of individual notes in a chord. At its simplest this meant that you could bring to the foreground the successive entries of a fugue theme, or make a melody sing out over a harmonic accompaniment, without having to make use of different manuals and registers as with a harpsichord. If a player could really master the operation of this new machine there would open up an infinitely variable and subtle expressive potential that would grow ever more as the piano developed. Yet almost a hundred years after Cristofori's first piano there were still piano owners who were ignorant of how to play the instrument properly.

Composers too were slow in grasping the potential of the new invention. There is no known music published specifically for the piano before a set of sonatas by an Italian composer, Lodovico Giustini, dated 1732. Although these have interesting dynamic markings like *piano . . . più piano . . . forte*, they are still written very much like harpsichord pieces and in no way exploit the capacities and characteristics of the fortepiano. The different dynamic markings relate to different phrases

32

*Part of a sonata by Giustini. See page 32.*

*Cristofori Piano with action taken out.*

Americus Backers 1772. See page 37.

Harpsichord with Venetian Swell, 1800.
Joseph Kirckman. See page 40.

or sections of the music, perhaps to the softer repeating of a phrase already played loud. There is no indication, for example, that Giustini expected the player to get progressively louder or softer *during* a phrase of music. J. S. Bach, who died in 1750, wrote nothing for the fortepiano, nor did Domenico Scarlatti, the great virtuoso and prolific composer for the keyboard, who lived till 1757; indeed it wasn't until about the last quarter of the century, and more than sixty years after Cristofori's first instrument, that music really suitable for the piano was being written.

Besides this Leipzig instrument there are two other Cristofori fortepianos surviving. One, made in 1720 and the earliest known, is in New York, but its present soundboard is not the original one and it is therefore of less interest as an example of Cristofori's own work. The other, made in 1722, is in Rome. It seems that Cristofori probably stopped making pianos after about 1726 (by which time it is estimated he had made about twenty) and returned to harpsichord construction until he died in 1731. Could it be that he was disheartened by the small response to the piano idea in his time? Could it be that the Italians, in love with the human voice and the violin, could not quite come to terms with the need for complex machinery between the player's fingers and the vibrating elements? Whatever the case, Cristofori was the first, and for our purposes the last, Italian piano-maker.

However, the idea had already been taken up in Germany by an organ-builder called Gottfried Silbermann. It appears that at one time he had the job of maintaining Pantaleon Hebenstreit's famous outsize dulcimer, and he was certainly aware of the possibilities of a stringed instrument using hammers. But the real impetus probably came from the Maffei article already mentioned, which was published in a German translation by Johann Ulrich von Koenig in 1725. Silbermann must have seen this, since a year later he produced two Grand fortepianos with an action clearly based on that of Cristofori. Some time later, probably about 1736, these instruments were shown to J. S. Bach who was not at all enthusiastic. How much this was due to failings in the instruments and how much to Bach's conservative nature it would be difficult to say, particularly since the instruments themselves haven't survived. Anyway, Silbermann persisted and later built more pianos, several of which were owned by Frederick the Great of Prussia. When Bach visited the King in 1747 he was shown these wonderful new acquisitions and again had the chance to try them. He is said to have praised the instruments this time, but as an employed musician in the presence of a King perhaps he could hardly have said anything else on such an occasion. The fact is that Bach was now over sixty and, for whatever reason, he didn't choose to write anything for the Forte and Piano.

Three of Silbermann's pianos of this period have survived, and it is known that they are based on Cristofori's design of 1726. In due course piano design was to take a slightly different course in South Germany, but the next stages in the development of Cristofori's action took place in England.

# 4
# England

The first fifty years of the fortepiano up to about 1760 had seen relatively slow progress. They had seen the development of a practical instrument; both the small domestic square piano and a vertical instrument had been realised, as we shall see later. And yet the idea of the fortepiano still hadn't really caught on. Its status tended to vary between that of interesting curiosity and unsatisfactory competitor with the harpsichord. The next fifty years, however, were to see a very dramatic change in this situation, and it was through the co-incidence of several different factors that the next part of the story took place in England.

In one sense this is surprising, since England had never been much of a harpsichord-making country. It is probable that most harpsichords used here since the sixteenth century had been imported, first from Northern Italy and then from Flemish makers, and those that *were* made here were derived from Italian or Flemish models. But in the 1720s and 1730s two names began to emerge: Jacob Kirckman and Burkat Shudi. Kirckman was a German from Bischweiler, near Strasbourg, who came to London in the 1720s as a young apprentice. Shudi was a Swiss joiner who also came to London when the problem of deforestation in his native Glarus forced many woodworkers into the new trade of cotton-weaving. Both these men started working for a harpsichord-maker called Tabel. Each in time set up his own independent harpsichord-making business, Shudi in about 1729, and Kirckman in 1738, having first married Tabel's widow. For the rest of the century these two men had a virtual monopoly of the harpsichord in England, and the instruments they made were very fine indeed. A considerable number of them still survive. Shudi and Kirckman became well-known figures in London life. Shudi was often visited by Handel, and he had a Royal Appointment to the Prince of Wales who owned one of his harpsichords. Another of his instruments went to Frederick the Great of Prussia, and the nine-year-old Mozart played a Shudi harpsichord in Potsdam.

By 1760 the fortepiano had been heard of in London: there is a story that one had actually been made by an English monk in Rome as early as 1711, and later brought to London, but there is no existing instrument to prove the point. A square piano was brought to England from Germany in 1755, though the maker's name isn't known.

Then things happened in quick succession. In 1759 Johann Christian Bach, son of J. S., came to London. Shortly after there arrived a number of continental instrument-makers whose harpsichord- and piano-building in Saxony had been effectively ended by the Seven Years War. One of these, Johannes Zumpe, had been a pupil of Silbermann and brought with him useful knowledge of the latest developments in fortepiano-making. Zumpe joined the business of Burkat Shudi. Another arrival in London, this time from Scotland, was a young man called John Broadwood, who had just completed his apprenticeship as a cabinet-maker. He too went to work for Shudi. Zumpe set up on his own after a few years and devoted himself to making small square pianos. Broadwood stayed on, married Shudi's daughter in 1769, and by the following year was in partnership with his father-in-law.

Meanwhile, in 1768, J. C. Bach had given the first public solo performance on a piano in London – actually on one of Zumpe's square pianos which had cost him £50. Bach was by now music teacher to Queen Charlotte, wife of George III, and his known preference for the fortepiano over the harpsichord, coupled with his Royal patronage, gave a powerful impetus to the new instrument. Also England had led the way in the growth of public concerts. Starting as tavern entertainments in the mid-seventeenth century they had become more like our idea of concerts when a London violinist, John Banister, in 1672 started organising performances which people could pay to hear. During the eighteenth century the concert-giving business steadily grew, and when the piano began to emerge as a desirable instrument it came to be increasingly in demand for public performance.

About the same time as Bach's concert, an apprentice of Broadwood's, Robert Stodart, was working with an instrument-maker called Americus Backers on the idea of a large harpsichord-shaped fortepiano with an improved version of the Cristofori action. Backers was a Dutchman and yet another of the makers who came over to London in about 1760. His fortepiano of 1772, made for the Duke of Wellington and still owned by the present Duke, is one of the earliest to survive. It is now kept in the Russell Collection at Edinburgh University. It is already a much more solid-looking affair than the Cristofori. Just as Cristofori's resembles the small Italian harpsichord in appearance, Backers' resembles in shape and size the harpsichords that Shudi and Kirckman were making. The frame is still entirely of wood, but of much heavier construction than Cristofori's. The sound of the instrument also is heavier and more powerful, but with the characteristic 'jangle' of the early fortepianos. The hammers are still small with slender wooden heads tipped with leather.

Another feature of this Backers fortepiano deserves particular mention. Like the Cristofori it has the *una corda* stop, but it also has a 'sustaining' stop, whereby all the dampers can be lifted from the strings with one control, leaving all the strings free to continue vibrating even after the keys have been released. And both these effects are controlled by foot pedals. Pedals had been fitted to harpsichords before (by Johannes Haward or John Hayward in England in the seventeenth century), but this is the first piano known to have them. They are fitted one to each of the two front legs of the instrument.

In spite of the more solid build of this Backers fortepiano it suffers from the same problems that were present in Cristofori's and that were to exercise increasingly the minds of piano-makers. There were three problems that were closely linked together: to make a louder instrument with a 'fuller' tone you would need to use larger, heavier hammers; but the strings would need to be stronger—that is thicker—to sustain the heavier blow; and then these thicker strings would have to be pulled tighter to keep the same pitch, and this increase of tension imposed on the wooden frame would twist it, and in time probably break it. There was a way out of the vicious circle, but this would have involved the use of iron and the piano-makers of the eighteenth century were not prepared to consider it. There was a general feeling that wood had a soul while iron did not, and also that metal would be irreparably damaging to the piano's tone. The resistance to its use was therefore powerful. So the success story of the English fortepiano is the story of an instrument with these problems largely unsolved.

38

By the 1770s the firm of Shudi and Broadwood was set for a period of enormous development. It was the presence of Zumpe and Stodart in Shudi's workshop that provided the spark for the growth of English piano-making, and the genius of John Broadwood that fuelled the fire. The older Shudi died in 1773 and was succeeded by his son, also called Burkat. But John Broadwood was now in control. The firm's first known piano is a square of 1780 labelled Shudi & Broadwood, but in 1782 the instruments are signed John Broadwood. The first Broadwood Grand fortepiano was made about 1786.

So, three-quarters of the way through the eighteenth century the business of making pianos was being established, and the desire to hear and own them stimulated. The growth of that desire and the means of its fulfilment were given enormous impetus by the great social changes that were taking place. The Industrial Revolution was at the centre of the forces that made possible the massive expansion in the manufacture and use of the piano. For one thing, the population of England rose from six and a half million in 1750 to nine million in 1800, fourteen million in 1830, and eighteen million in 1850. Meanwhile improved methods of production meant more goods produced and consequently greater wealth for the people who owned these means of production. So there grew up a new middle class with aspirations to a higher social status. But old-established clubs don't willingly accept new upstart members, and money on its own was not enough to secure elevation to the ranks of gentlefolk, particularly if the money had been acquired through trade.

The piano, we have seen, was becoming fashionable, and the possession of a fortepiano came to be a symbol of social status. (J. C. Bach's London concerts were made even more desirable by allowing only a limited number of subscribers.) One advantage of the piano from this viewpoint was that playing it was plainly a useless occupation. There could not accrue to the player any taint of work or labour – provided of course that he were not so ill-advised as to take the occupation too seriously. Or rather one should say 'she', since playing the fortepiano was always regarded, in fashionable society at least, as being essentially a pastime for ladies.

The harpsichord meanwhile was fighting a considerable rearguard action. English harpsichords had become very big – up to nine feet long compared with a more normal seven feet on the continent. They had already developed a complex system of stops to provide different tone colours. As the piano threat grew a few last frenzied attempts were made to compete with the newer instrument's sensitive dynamic control. In 1769 Shudi patented a Venetian swell which covered the strings and sounding-board and which could be opened and shut like a Venetian blind. The device was operated by a pedal, and of course enabled a crescendo and diminuendo effect to be produced. Kirckman some years earlier had already fitted his 'nag's head swell', whereby a hinged section of the lid was opened and closed by a pedal, again allowing crescendo and diminuendo. One French inventor patented a system for progressively moving the jack registers closer to or farther from the strings, so that the plectra would pluck more or less strongly at the control of the player. Another more desperate Frenchman tried to simulate the sounds of other instruments, and even the human voice, on his harpsichord.

But the composers and performers were not to be

seduced by even the more musical of these devices. Between 1733 and 1764 the great harpsichord composers Couperin, J. S. Bach, Domenico Scarlatti, Handel, Rameau all died. The new generation had other ideas. Mozart, born in 1756, played the harpsichord when young but was soon to declare his allegiance to the piano, as did Haydn, 24 years his senior. The younger Shudi made his last harpsichord in 1793. The end, when it came, was quick. Harpsichords were soon being ruthlessly destroyed, and when Broadwoods were offered one in part exchange in 1802 they replied that 'from their almost total disuse they are unsaleable'.

The names of the great eighteenth-century composers are now so familiar that one sometimes needs reminding that they are almost all from Germany, France and Italy. Towards the end of the century there was a great influx into England of continental musicians, partly because of the unsettled state of revolutionary France where many of them were working, and partly, no doubt, because of the active developing concert scene in London. Haydn visited London in 1791 and directed performances of his orchestral works from the piano. Not so long before this would always have been done from the harpsichord.

The keyboard's function in orchestral music had always been to fill out the harmonic structure of the music, and the director would sit with his back to the audience so that he could face the musicians and conduct them from the keyboard. A significant change in position of the fortepiano in public performance is attributed to another continental visitor, Jan Ladislav Dussek. Dussek was a composer and pianist of great public popularity in London in the last decade of the century, and he is said to have been the first to sit with his profile to the audience. The emotional temperature of the keyboard player's 'presence' is beginning to rise. By this time the piano concertos of Mozart were becoming known and the piano had become a popular solo instrument. Mozart's orchestral music, and Haydn's too, were also becoming very popular in England. Around the turn of the century, there grew up a craze for piano versions of these orchestral works, usually for two people playing at one piano. This in turn helped to generate the need for a greater keyboard range, and for some time this was provided by what were known as 'additional keys'. These were first introduced on the square piano in 1794 and, as we shall see with the domestic piano (see p. 71), they represent a means of adding extra notes to the top end of the piano's range. The range of the Grand piano was increased too. Dussek had Broadwood's first six-octave Grand in 1794, and by 1800 five and a half or six were the norm on Grands.

Then the Waltz, which was imported from Vienna in the 1790s, began a vogue in England and the new piano-owners naturally wished to play this music and dance to it. The piano was becoming more than just a fashionable toy. For the people who could afford to buy one it was a real living force in the culture and entertainment of their homes.

As demand was created, the means of satisfying it was not neglected. A major factor in the growth of the piano business was the use of that product of the Industrial Revolution, the factory system. The piano was an ideal candidate for this process in which each man makes a part of the object and all the parts are assembled at the end of a production line. The piano consists of a large number of individual parts, and each part of the action of the piano, for example, could be made in large numbers by one man. The keyboard too might be made separately. Hitchpins, wrest pins and bridge pins (to keep the strings in place on the bridge) would also be needed in large numbers. Meanwhile a skilled joiner could be making fortepiano cases, while others made soundboards, prepared sets of strings, or put together the completed instruments.

It was an aspect of John Broadwood's genius that he was quick to see the potential of this, and by applying factory methods he was able to push his output way above his continental rivals. In 1800 he made between 400 and 500 pianos compared with about fifty by his busiest Viennese competitor. By 1805 the total was well over 1000 a year. In the 1820s production of Grand fortepianos was running at about 340 a year, and of squares at about 1400. Against these figures it is sobering to realise that the entire Shudi output of harpsichords over sixty-five years was less than 1200.

There are a number of Broadwood's fortepianos from this period still surviving, and some of the best preserved – and very much still in playing order – are housed in the Colt Clavier Collection in Kent, probably the finest piano collection in Europe. There is, for example, a Grand of 1787, one of the earliest Broadwoods in playing order. There is an instrument of 1794 which is the same model as the three pianos that Haydn acquired when he was in London that year. It's intriguing to think that Haydn might have tried this very instrument when he was making his choice. Another Grand fortepiano, dated 1819, is the same model as that which Broadwoods presented to Beethoven in Vienna in 1817.

The difference in the sound of the 1787 fortepiano and that of 1819 is very noticeable. While they both sound essentially like fortepianos, the earlier one is very clear and bright, while the later is beginning to have

43

what one might call a fruitier quality – a little fuller
and rounder in tone, almost a little more conscious of
its dignity. Broadwood's Letter Book of 1800–10, containing copies of letters (mainly requests for payment!)
written during that period, provides some interesting
documentary evidence about the piano's status at the
time. For one thing, it is clear that their fortepianos
were going as far afield as Moscow and India. In reply
to a query from Denmark they explain that

the instrument the most fashionable here is the Grand Pianoforte,
sold retail at 70 guineas [the rapidly changing value of money
makes comparison difficult, but that would be more than £1500
now] in plain case and ornamental at 85 guineas . . . if you will,
permit us to send such an one.

There were also, it seems, some unscrupulous manufacturers, and Broadwoods had to write to a dis-
satisfied piano owner in India that the instrument being
complained of, though bearing the Broadwood sig-
nature, was not in fact of their make. There is evidence,
too, that after nearly 100 years of existence and some
thirty years of growing popularity in England the
particular qualities of the fortepiano were still often
misunderstood. One customer wrote requesting a
softer pedal and received the reply:

It has never been thought necessary, as the beauty of the instrument and which has caused it to supersede both the organ and
the harpsichord, has been thought to consist in the means it
affords the player of modulating its tones from piano to forte
by the delicacy of touch which is to be acquired by a little
practice.

In fact Broadwoods did, in 1810, and under protest,
make a Grand fortepiano with the Venetian swell
device as had been applied by Shudi to the harpsichord,
but it was not a trend they wished to encourage – nor
indeed was it necessary.

One might think from this correspondence that the
rapidly increasing popularity of the fortepiano took

Broadwoods themselves by surprise, for at one point we find them having to admit that 'from the great and unexpected demand we have none to sell'. Certainly some of the buyers had small ability – or perhaps little intention – of paying. Most of the reminders are extravagantly courteous, but there is a refreshing blast from the writer to Dr Baker of Derby: 'If you don't pay in a few days you will be arrested.'

Like Shudi's harpsichord firm before him, and indeed like any ambitious commercial operator, Broadwood made sure that his instruments were used by distinguished people. His firm retained the Royal Warranty, becoming Manufacturers 'to His Majesty and The Princesses' in 1800, and on Queen Victoria's accession in 1837 'Manufacturers to Her Majesty and The Royal Family'. We have seen that Haydn and Beethoven both had Broadwood fortepianos. In spite of his deafness Beethoven was particularly fond of his 1817 Broadwood, although its frame was made entirely of wood, and it was not really strong enough for the demands he made upon it. In fact major change was already in the air.

The problem of the strength of the wooden frame was becoming more and more acute for two reasons. The 'additional keys' already mentioned were subjecting the frame to increased tension, but at the same time the overall pitch of all instruments was being progressively raised. We accept today that middle C means the same note anywhere in the world. But this was not always the case. At one time there were different standards of pitch for different sorts of music, and for domestic keyboard instruments in the early seventeenth century middle C would have been as much as a tone and a half lower than it is today. By Mozart's day the normal pitch was about a semitone lower than ours, but there was an increasing tendency for the overall pitch to rise. This was particularly prompted by the demands of woodwind manufacturers who were raising the pitch of their instruments as part of the means of achieving a greater brilliance of tone. Naturally piano-makers had to follow suit, and for some time during the nineteenth century the standard pitch actually rose higher than today's. For the piano this meant that every single string had to be pulled tighter to achieve the required pitch, and this extra strain imposed on the wooden frame caused severe difficulties. Wooden bracing of the frame was tried, but this had to be so large to be effective that it tended to make the instrument unacceptably cumbersome. The use of iron in the frame at last became inevitable.

By 1808 Broadwoods were beginning to use metal tension bars in the treble to provide additional support for the frame, and in 1821 they were using between three and five such bars in their Grand pianos.

Another development in the use of metal was the compensation frame, which was intended to keep the instrument in tune through changes of temperature. Since metal expands as temperature rises and contracts as it falls, in a warmer atmosphere the strings of a piano will expand and therefore slacken, causing a lowering of pitch. And because some strings were of brass and some of steel, their rate of expansion or contraction was different. The principle of the compensation frame, which was invented by James Thom and William Allen, two workmen employed by William Stodart, was that by fixing metal tubes (thirteen in their patent of 1820) to each end of the frame, lying above and parallel to the strings, any expansion in the strings would be compensated for by a corresponding expansion of the tubes. Thus the same temperature change that would stretch and slacken the strings would also stretch the metal tubes and thereby restore the string tension. By having brass tubes above the brass strings and steel above the steel, their different rates of expansion were also allowed for. It was an ingenious device, and indeed it seems to have been successful, but in practical terms the most important requirement was still the strength of the frame to cope with the ever-increasing string tension.

It is perhaps somewhat unfair to have concentrated so much on the firm of Broadwoods. Rosamund Harding, in her *History of the Piano-Forte* (1933), lists well over 400 piano-makers who were working between 1760 and 1851 in London alone. But in spite of the contributions that were made by other English makers, the main credit for the supremacy of the English piano before 1830 rests on Broadwoods. One other manufacturer does deserve special mention, however. Although he was born in Rome in 1752, Muzio Clementi was brought to England as a boy of fourteen, and indeed became very much an English gentleman. He had started his career as a composer, pianist and teacher, but around 1800 he decided to go into piano-making with a group of others, and there emerged in due course the firm of Clementi and Co. At this point Clementi gave up playing the piano and shortly set out on a European trip that was to last some eight years.

On his return he resumed composition and produced the first Tutor for the piano that really comprehensively tackled the problems of piano technique. Indeed his sonata, op. 2 (1773), is regarded by many as the first piece of music that really matches the capacities of the piano. His Tutor, *Gradus ad Parnassum*, published in 1817, is still in use today. So the learning of technique as a function apart from the actual making of music became an accepted element in piano-teaching.

Clementi's firm, which after his death in 1832 was renamed Collard and Collard, was not a great innovator in its influence on the future development of the piano, but it did devise an effective means of securing the strings at the hitchpin, and it was applying the idea of enhancing the resonance of pianos by allowing extra lengths of vibrating string long before Steinways introduced the idea on the modern Grand (see p. 95). They were the biggest rivals to Broadwoods, and had the greater success on the American market. Their proportion of square pianos to Grands was considerably higher than Broadwoods' and a large number of their squares survive today. They also made many of the cabinet pianos described in Chapter 7, and their instruments tended to be more lavishly decorated.

Once the principle of reinforcing the wooden frame with iron had been established the way was opened up for a new phase in the development of piano sound. But parallel developments had already been taking place in Europe where for a time piano-makers had been following two quite separate paths.

Broadwood, 1787. See page 43.

John Broadwood (1732–1812)

*Broadwood, 1819. See page 43.*

*Broadwood, c. 1823 with
iron tension bars. See page 46.*

# 5
# Vienna

We have seen how in England the rise of the bourgeoisie
played an essential part in the growth of the piano's
popularity. The story was much the same all over
Europe. What varied from country to country was the
way the new middle class emerged. In Vienna, capital
of Austria and centre of the Great Habsburg Empire,
there was no sudden industrial expansion as in England,
or dramatic revolution as in France. But there was at
the end of the eighteenth century a very musical
Emperor, Joseph II, who was eccentrically 'liberal'.
Some of his ordinances were so extreme as to need
almost instant repealing, as for instance the decree of
1782 by which aristocrats and privy councillors guilty
of minor offences were punished by having to sweep
the streets. The new bourgeoisie that emerged during
his reign was made up largely of the bureaucrats and
professional men required to run the empire, though
there were of course traders too. Such people could
not afford the lavish musical establishments of their
aristocratic predecessors, but they could run musical
evenings of chamber music – hence all those trios and
quartets by Mozart, Haydn and Beethoven. And, as
elsewhere, they championed the piano. By 1781 the
instrument was so popular that Mozart, on a visit to
Vienna, could write, 'this is *clavierland*'.

As a status symbol the piano was relatively cheap.
Comparisons of costs across different periods of time
are notoriously unreliable, but one might hazard that
the range of the Viennese instruments ran from £350

to £1200 in today's money. This bought a new piano entirely built by craftsmen, the more expensive of which would have been beautifully decorated. The bottom end of the price range is similar to ours but one can easily pay over £3500 for a first-class instrument today.

No other European city has ever enjoyed the musical pre-eminence that was Vienna's between 1770 and 1830. The list of composers who either lived there or who went there to make their reputation reads like a musical 'Who's Who' of the period: Mozart, Haydn, Beethoven, Czerny, Schubert, Schumann, Chopin, to mention only the most famous. It was at this time a musical Mecca and, not surprisingly, it evolved its own particular kind of piano – one in which the action was fundamentally different in construction from its English counterpart.

The 'Viennese' action is actually a misnomer since it was first developed by a South German, Johann Andreas Stein, who was born in Augsburg in 1728. Mozart visited his workshops there and greatly admired his instruments. He wrote to his father:

Stein it is true does not sell his pianos for less than 300 florins but the care and work he puts into them is beyond price . . . I can do with the keys what I like – the tone is always equal. It does not tinkle disagreeably. It has neither the fault of being too loud or too soft – nor does it fail entirely – in a word the tone is perfectly equal throughout . . . his pianos are really solid. He gives a guarantee that the soundboard will neither break nor crack – when he has finished the soundboard of a piano he exposes it to the air, to the rain, to snow, to the heat of the sun, to every imaginable devilry in order to make it crack. Then he glues in slivers of wood so that it becomes completely solid and resistant. . . .[1]

Stein later moved to Vienna and on his death his business was continued by his sons. Meanwhile his daughter, Nanette, married Johann Andreas Streicher

[1] Quoted in E. Closson, *History of the Piano* (Elek, 1947).

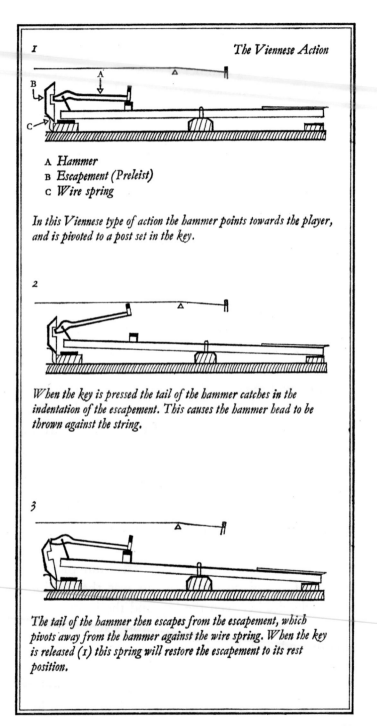

*The Viennese Action*

**1**

A *Hammer*
B *Escapement (Preleist)*
C *Wire spring*

In this Viennese type of action the hammer points towards the player, and is pivoted to a post set in the key.

**2**

When the key is pressed the tail of the hammer catches in the indentation of the escapement. This causes the hammer head to be thrown against the string.

**3**

The tail of the hammer then escapes from the escapement, which pivots away from the hammer against the wire spring. When the key is released (*1*) this spring will restore the escapement to its rest position.

and together they started the firm of Nanette Streicher (née Stein). Beethoven owned a Streicher, still to be seen in Vienna. The number of piano-makers in Vienna rose rapidly. The names worth remembering are those that we can ally to specific composers. Anton Walter built a piano for Mozart in 1784, the year Mozart wrote six piano concertos and his big Sonata in C minor, K 457. J. Wenzel Schanz built one for Haydn in 1788, and Conrad Graf one for Beethoven in 1824 (see p. 56).

What then was so different about the Viennese piano? In its early years it was a delicate-looking instrument, not unlike a small harpsichord in appearance. By the second decade of the nineteenth century it looked much more solid, with a deeper case and thicker, rounded legs. Its compass in 1770 was only five octaves, from the F two and a half octaves below middle C to the F two and a half octaves above it. It did not expand to five and a half octaves until the time of Beethoven's Third Piano Concerto. At first it had no foot pedals – the *una corda* and the dampers were activated by knee-levers built on the underside of the case: Mozart was one of the first to insist on foot pedals for his Walter in 1784. From then on the pedals proliferated and later Viennese pianos had as many as five for various extra effects, such as little bells, drums and a row of parchment which lay across the bass strings to make what was called a 'bassoon' effect.

What set these instruments apart from the mainstream of the piano development was their action – the mechanics between the key and the hammer. One can trace a direct line from Cristofori's action, through Broadwood and Erard (see p. 60), to our modern Grand pianos. The Viennese action worked on a quite different, far simpler principle: the hammers all pointed towards the player, instead of away from him as in all other actions, and they were permanently attached to the key, pinned into a U-shaped piece of brass screwed into the key. When the key was depressed, the hammer was set in motion by its tail, which protruded, flicking a rail permanently fixed along the whole length of the action. After the flick the tail passed over the rail or 'escaped'. It was all beautifully simple – no notches or hopper levers. The result was an action which had a very shallow key depression and was extremely light. The hammers were covered in leather (as were all hammers at the time) and very small, so Viennese string tended to be on the thin side.

The sound of the Viennese piano is so completely different from that of our modern Grand that it can cause quite a shock. While, in the broadest terms, it is similar to that made by the English Broadwoods and French Erards of the period, familiarity soon makes one appreciate its distinctive timbre – silvery, fragile, and yet with great carrying power and clarity of line. Moreover, the relationship between its various registers, the bottom, the middle and the top, is quite different from that of today's instruments. To play Mozart, Haydn or early Beethoven on one is to feel difficulties of balance and legato disappear under one's fingers: the melodies sing out over the accompaniment and all that famous Beethoven 'muddiness' in the bass never occurs. The lightness and shallowness of the key depression even makes all those awkward ornaments easier, and there is no feeling of containment or restraint as there is when playing this music on a modern instrument with a seven-and-a-half-octave compass. Mozart, Haydn, and Beethoven frequently used the entire compass of their five- or five-and-a-half-octave instruments. Mozart would organise his scale passages so that, regardless of the key they were in, they would go up to the very top note of the instrument so as to make use of the full range of the keyboard. When these passages are played on a modern instrument they leave a margin of unused notes which create a feeling of unexploited resources. Played on an instrument of Mozart's time they give the feeling of stretching the instrument to its utmost and releasing its full resonance. As a result such passages feel bigger even though played on a smaller instrument.

But the most important result of all is that playing these instruments changes one's whole conception of the music of the period. These pianos still have a jangling percussiveness more akin to the harpsichord than to the somewhat glutinous tone of our modern instruments. The drama this can create is enormous. Since the sound is drier there is less temptation to string all the phrases into unending legato lines; for this was surely the age when musical ideas came in carefully, even if instinctively, balanced short units.[1]

[1] The whole question of late eighteenth-century phrasing is an enormous one and only marginally relevant to this book. Yet having raised the point it is worth a cursory if possibly inadequate example. A comparison between the Urtext's (and therefore Mozart's) phrasing of the opening of the first movement of the Sonata in F, K332, with that given in the Peters Edition published in the late 1800s makes the point:

(*a*) Henle Urtext Edition

(*b*) Peters (Köhler & Schmidt) Edition

The whole beauty of Mozart's slurring is the feeling of balance it creates between any one bar and the next: one interval up, the other down. The interruption of the pattern of the first three bars by the quaver slur which starts the fourth heightens the feeling of suspension on E, the leading note. To phrase the four bars in one unending tune is to destroy all this subtlety. Yet nearly all late 19th-century editors felt entitled to obliterate Mozart's detailed slurring and replace it with long lines. One can see why it happened: theirs was the age of Bruckner and Wagner.

The sustaining pedal becomes virtually a colouring device and the *una corda* really does move the hammers to hit only *one* string, making possible a complete spectrum of timbres. The whole instrument has little resonance or power to sustain and so, not surprisingly, one finds few chordal or sustained passages in Mozart or Haydn.

Even in Beethoven's time the Viennese piano was fighting for survival against its English competitors. The English piano had more power and resonance and was proving more in keeping with the tempestuousness of the emerging romantic temperament. Viennese methods of piano production were less advanced, in the factory sense, than England's (Streicher was producing only fifty a year at the turn of the century). Add to this English sales acumen and a shift of musical interest to Paris in the 1840s and it is not difficult to see why the Viennese piano disappeared from the musical scene. Yet for the music written with its sound in mind it has no peer, and our modern piano is a very poor substitute. True, its fragility caused problems, even at the time. Anton Reicha told how he assisted, in a somewhat unusual fashion, at a performance of Beethoven's:

One day Beethoven played at Court a concerto by Mozart and he asked me to turn the pages for him. At every moment the strings of the instrument kept snapping and jumping into the air while the hammers got entangled in the broken strings. Beethoven wishing to finish the piece at all costs begged me to disengage the hammers and to remove the broken strings whenever he paused in playing. My job was harder than his for I had constantly to jump to the right and the left to run around the piano to get at all the troubles.[1]

Johann Stumphe, after a visit to Beethoven, described the state of his piano:

What a spectacle offered itself to my view – there was no sound in the treble and broken strings were mixed up like a thorn bush after a gale.[2]

[1] Clossan *op. cit.*     [2] *Ibid.*

Conrad Graf built Beethoven a piano in 1824 and tried to give it more volume by stringing each note with four strings instead of the usual three. The instrument still exists, in playing order, in the Beethoven house in Bonn. The fourth string did not prove to be the answer: the instrument is no louder than the Broadwoods of the period. In any case Beethoven died three years later and wrote nothing more for piano between the instrument's arrival and his death.

The whole evolution of the Viennese piano made it impossible to modify it to take the pounding romantic pianists wanted to give their instruments. The problem had to be solved elsewhere. This is why the story of the Viennese piano is the story of a vital cul-de-sac.

To us, retrospectively, the late eighteenth-century Viennese piano repertoire appears to consist of the concertos, sonatas, rondos and variations of Haydn, Mozart and Beethoven, but in fact this is only a small part of it. These were the early days of public concerts and their programmes were very different from today's. The solo recital was still unknown. A concert involving a pianist centred round a concerto, usually written by him, possibly some songs which he might accompany, and then the almost obligatory improvisation on some popular tunes, frequently from the latest opera that was all the rage. The sonatas, rondos and variations that form the core of present-day piano-recital programmes were played exclusively in people's homes on semi-private occasions.

The piano was the focal centre of music in the home. Whatever the latest musical craze, its products would be transcribed and simplified for people to play at home. As music moved out of the palaces it inevitably began to contain more popular elements. At about this time the operetta or 'Singspiel' became very popular and provided an endless supply of catchy tunes to serve as themes for a veritable industry of variation writers.

Also about this time the Waltz came to Vienna. It had originally been a rustic dance. But Walzen means revolving and to do this with any security one has to clasp one's partner closely. 'How disgusting!' muttered the older generation, as they have so often done throughout history; nevertheless Vienna became the city of the waltz and hundreds of waltzes were written or transcribed for piano.

The piano has always lent itself to the painting of musical pictures; it is a good creator of sound effects. Descriptive music became very popular – music telling stories, depicting storms or other natural phenomena. There were battle pieces, often meticulously labelled to represent the roar of cannons, the charges, the groans of the dying. Then there was also a Turkish craze about this time – Mozart's opera 'Die Entführung aus dem Serail' exploited it. The Ottoman empire reached up to Vienna's doorstep: the music of the period mirrored it. The Viennese piano with its bells and drum jangled its way merrily through pseudo-Turkish pieces such as Mozart's 'Rondo alla Turca'.

Undoubtedly the bulk of the music played on those Viennese pianos was mere entertaining rubbish. And yet there must have been something very special about Vienna between 1770 and 1830 for it produced compositions that are in many people's minds the yardstick for what they consider 'great' in music; possibly the greatest single flowering in the history of our music.

# 6
# Paris

There is a fascinating contrast of attitudes to music between the Teutons and the Latins. The German-speaking peoples often approach it almost devotionally as one of the ways of explaining life itself. Bach in the *B minor Mass*, for instance, used musical techniques to illustrate the relationship between God the Father and God the Son: Beethoven wrote a great Hymn to Joy.

To the French music means something quite differ-ent and we Anglo-Saxons can find it somewhat of an enigma. It is almost as if the French temperament has always been more concerned with *how* a work of art is realised than what it stands for or represents in con-ceptual terms. Since earliest times French composers have chosen descriptive, almost trivial, names for their pieces. Their eighteenth-century harpsichord reper-toire is full of titles such as 'The Little Windmills'; 'The Cyclops'; 'The Swallow'. Debussy, a prolific piano composer, never wrote a piano sonata, that main-stay of the Germanic pianistic repertoire. The French creative artist, immensely sensitive and skilled, revels in the sensual satisfaction of his craft and seems to fight shy of those heavy imponderables so beloved by his Teutonic neighbours. The Frenchman's quick mer-curial imagination grasps many potentialities that his impatience obliges him to leave to others to exploit. France boasts an impressive list of 'firsts' in artistic concepts and techniques. Even in the story of the piano they were among the prime movers. A century before Cristofori a Frenchman experimented with a hammer-struck dulcimer but he solved none of the basic problems of the action and the French dropped out of the story for nearly 200 years, to return to the scene thanks to Sebastien Erard – originally spelt Erhard – born German and strongly influenced by the English.

Paris was amongst the first cities to give public concerts – the famous Concerts Spirituels started in 1725. These were primarily concerts of sacred music and took place only on holy days in the church calendar. Everything had to be sung in Latin. Their promoter, a Monsieur Philidor, held a licence (which cost him 10,000 livres a year) entitling him to put these concerts on in a hall in the Tuileries and charge admission for them, the proceeds then being his. They were soon prestigious social events.

Music-making in bourgeois and aristocratic homes was widespread before even the revolution and Napoleon's cataclysmic wars. After them it took Parisians time to settle down again but by the 1830s their glittering salons and musical soirées were the prototypes and envy of the world. They bred a special species of pianist, the 'salonist' – epitomised by the good-looking Henri Herz – a species very much in Schumann's mind when he wrote of the Philistines. Paris, however, was also the home of Chopin and Liszt, not to mention a host of less familiar but nevertheless brilliant virtuosi and, as with Vienna earlier, it was only natural that it should develop its own school of piano-makers.

The French harpsichord had reached a peak under Pascal Taskin (1723–93), instrument-maker to the King. Towards the end of his life he began making pianos but his instruments made little impression on a market strongly dominated by the English. Sebastien Erard, born in Strasbourg in 1752, had moved to Paris when he was sixteen. He built his first piano – a square – in 1777. Soon afterwards he opened his own shop in partnership with his brother but had to appeal to the King when in 1786 his jealous competitors seized the shop and closed it. He was granted a royal 'Brevet' or licence and continued making square pianos until he fled to London during the Reign of Terror. There he set up a factory in Kensington and was much influenced by the work of the Broadwoods – for instance, he used the English action.

In 1796 he returned to Paris and took up his business again. He now started making Grand pianos. His father had been a cabinet-maker and Sebastien had started in his workshop, so that his pianos have all the elegance of the French Premier Empire style with those characteristic tapering legs and gilding. The sound of his early Grands was somewhat similar to a Broadwood, only perhaps slightly more 'nasal'. Beethoven had one of these early Erards in 1803, about the time he was writing his third and fourth Piano Concertos and the *Waldstein* and *Appassionata* Sonatas.

Erard was responsible for three important improvements to the piano. The first two, patented in 1809, were the 'agraffe' and the 'celeste'. There is one agraffe to each note. It is a small piece of metal with three holes in it through which the strings pass at the keyboard end before they are wound onto the wrest pins. Together with the wrest pins, it is screwed into the wrest plank, and its function is to produce an upward bearing by the strings at this point. (All previous methods had produced a downward bearing.) Since the hammers strike upwards at this end of the string, an upward bearing helps attenuate the effects of the hammer blow. The agraffe was a little before its time,

61

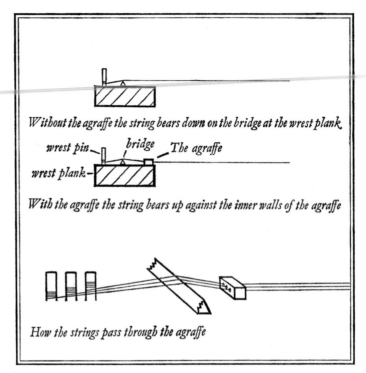

*Without the agraffe the string bears down on the bridge at the wrest plank.*

wrest pin— *bridge* The agraffe

wrest plank—

*With the agraffe the string bears up against the inner walls of the agraffe*

*How the strings pass through the agraffe*

however. In the early stages, being screwed into the wood of the wrest plank, it could work loose. It was not until they were fixed into the cast-iron frame that they realised their full potential, and they are now almost universally used. The celeste, otherwise called the 'sourdine', was a strip of felt attached to a bar brought across between the hammers and the strings by means of a pedal. It made a very noticeable change in the timbre. Though this device has never caught on to any extent, it is still found in some French uprights and frequently used for semi-silent practice.

Erard's greatest contribution to piano design, however, was his 'double escapement' action, patented in 1821. As we have seen, escapement is the basic essential of the piano action. With a point of escapement, however contrived, the hammer mechanism can complete the two movements towards the string and away from

62

it while the key has made only one downward movement. To repeat that same note the key must be allowed
right up to its original starting position so that the rest
of the action can realign itself so as to start again. This
limits the speed of repetition. Erard realised that by
adding a second point of escapement he could get a
note to repeat without the key having to go more than
halfway back to its original starting position. Exactly
how he did this is complex, so its detailed explanation
is left to an appendix (see pp. 108-9).

The addition of a second escapement not only increased the speed at which notes could be repeated
but gave the piano what is often called its 'second
touch'. This means playing a note from about halfway
down its key's descent, thereby reducing key movement
and acceleration, and gaining far greater control in soft
passages. It was yet another factor giving the pianist
a wider range of control over the sound he makes.
The inclusion of two escapements is technically impossible in the Viennese action, another strong reason
for its total disappearance.

Sebastien Erard died in 1831 but his nephew Pierre
had already been in the business for some years and
he took it over on his uncle's death. Pierre Erard himself died in 1855 and was in turn succeeded by his
widow. After her death the business passed into the
hands of someone who had married into the family.
The London branch stopped trading in 1890, though
a hall bearing the firm's name survived in Great
Marlborough Street, London, right into modern times.
The firm now no longer exists: it was finally wound up
in 1971. As a footnote it is worth mentioning that
Sebastien Erard was also responsible for perfecting
the design of the modern harp.

The other world-famous French piano is the Pleyel.

Ignace Pleyel, born in 1757 in Austria, was a composer and a favourite pupil of Haydn. After a stay in Italy, he became Kapellmeister at Strasbourg Cathedral, during which time he also conducted in London. By 1800 he had moved to Paris and started a music-selling business and in 1807 he founded his piano factory. As Clementi had done earlier in London, he abandoned an active musical career to become a businessman.

From the very outset Pleyel employed Henri Pape to organise his factory. Pape was an extremely ingenious and imaginative piano designer. He experimented with the shape of the piano; he built them round, oval and hexagonal; he produced a table model; he tried downward striking hammers; he stretched the keyboard's compass to eight octaves (most modern Grands only have seven and a half). All these experiments are now only curiosities. But one invention of Pape's is fundamental to the modern piano's sound. In 1826 he patented the use of felt for covering hammers. It took some decades before leather coverings were to disappear completely, and there was an intermediary stage when felt cores were covered with a thin layer of leather, but in time leather disappeared completely and with it disappeared the last vestiges of the old fortepiano's sound.

Ignace Pleyel, being himself a musician, was able to keep his links with the profession. A well-known pianist, Friedrich Kalkbrenner, joined his business in 1824; Chopin greatly admired Pleyel's instrument, and played several times in Pleyel's Concert Rooms. Camille Pleyel, Ignace's eldest son, went into partnership with his father in 1821 and took over the business on his father's death ten years later. He was a friend of Chopin and not only supplied him with pianos but acted frequently on his behalf in the publication of his

*Stodart, c. 1825 with compensation frame.*
*See page 46.*

*Viennese Grand with five pedals*
*and special effects, c. 1820. See page 57.*

*Johann Andreas Stein*, 1728–1792. *See page* 50.

*Fortepiano*, 1802 *by André Stein,*
*son of Johann Andreas.*

*Sebastien Erard*, 1752–1851. *See page* 60.

*Erard Grand Piano, c.* 1868. *See page* 66.

*Ignace Pleyel,* 1757–1831. *See page* 64.

*Pleyel Grand Piano,* 1828. *See page* 66.

music. After Camille's death in 1855 the family lost control of the business, but the firm still exists today.

By now the whole musical scene had changed. Gone were those restrained, elegant ensembles playing in aristocratic houses. The orchestra had doubled its size to be able to cope with works like the Symphonie Fantastique by Berlioz. Romanticism was, in one of its aspects, the cult of the individual. The individual in performance is the virtuoso and Paganini, the father of them all, began mesmerising his audiences with his fiddle-playing. Pianists were soon to follow suit. One thinks immediately of Liszt and Chopin, because their compositions are still played. But there were many others: some who lived there, some merely passing through – Moscheles, Thalberg, Kalkbrenner, Alkan, Litolf, Dreyschock, Henselt, to mention only the most famous. Moscheles may have been the first pianist ever to give a complete solo recital – in London in 1837: Liszt also claimed the privilege in Rome in 1839. Virtuosi sprang up everywhere, touring Europe and receiving something of the adulation we reserve today for our pop stars. When Liszt was in Berlin in 1842 he rode in a carriage drawn by six white horses, escorted by thirty other carriages and hundreds of private coaches.

The piano was desperately trying to keep pace with the increasing demands made on it. In Liszt's early career he virtually demolished a piano in one item and it was nothing for him to require two or three instruments to be able to complete the programme. Beethoven, as we know, had done much the same thing. The pianos of the early 1800s were expressive, but the romantics wanted power as well. The problem of providing them with it centred round the frame to which the strings were attached. Erard's double-escapement English

E

action could carry a far larger hammer than the earlier fortepianos had; yet the strings simply could not take the blows pianists like Liszt wanted to give them.

As we saw in Chapter 2, the pitch of a note depends on how tightly a string is stretched. And there is the other factor – the string's thickness. The thicker it is the more tightly it must be stretched to produce any given note, and consequently the greater the strain on the frame on to which it is strung. In the early stages piano-makers resisted the idea of putting iron into their instruments. Nearly all other musical instruments were made of wood, and they felt iron would alter the sound. But iron crept into piano manufacture bit by bit nevertheless. We have already come across its use by English makers, particularly Broadwoods. By 1830 both Pleyels and Erards were using tension bars, running along the length of at least part of the frame. They were also beginning to use metal plating into which to seat the hitchpins holding the strings. There is an Erard of 1868 in the Colt Clavier Collection very much of the same design as the pianos owned by Liszt and Wagner. It has wrought-iron tension bars running the full length of the frame every ten inches or so across its width. The frame itself is entirely of cast iron but made in sections bolted together. The instrument sounds surprisingly modern but its complicated compromise solution to the framing problem was to be superseded by someone who would uninhibitedly use cast iron. This was unlikely to happen in traditionalist Europe. The Americans were to provide the lasting solution.

# 7
# *The Domestic Piano*

So far the story of the piano has been told almost exclusively in terms of the Grand, which has always represented the best example at any point in the piano's history. Yet more than two million of the privately owned pianos in Britain are uprights while only just over a hundred thousand are Grands. This means that one household in every eight or nine has an upright piano. And it is on the domestic instrument that the commercial success of the piano industry rests.

We have already seen that there were small-sized domestic keyboard instruments before the piano was invented. But although some earlier attempts to produce a hammer-action keyboard instrument seem to have been made along the lines of the dulcimer and the clavichord, the first known successful piano was firmly based on the conception of the harpsichord. In short, the first piano was a Grand in everything but name. But it didn't take long for inventive piano-makers to set their minds to the job of building something that took up less space. In fact the first known upright piano, by an unknown maker, is thought to date from 1735, twenty-six years after Cristofori's first instrument. To the casual eye this looks just like a harpsichord stuck up on end with its tail in the air.

The basic idea of converting a horizontal instrument into a vertical one was not new. The harpsichord is known to have received this treatment at the beginning of the seventeenth century, producing an amazing instrument called a 'clavicytherium'. And the French maker Jean Marius, who was working on the hammer keyboard idea early in the eighteenth century, submitted models for four 'Clavecins à Maillets' (or keyboard instruments with hammers) to the Académie Royale des Sciences de Paris in 1716, of which one was an upright. But these don't seem to have aroused great interest and nothing more is heard of them.

In fact, any upright form of piano presents certain problems of design, since the up-and-down motion of the keys, which in a Grand relate to an up-and-down motion of hammers striking horizontal strings, in the upright has to be transmitted into a backwards-and-forwards motion of hammers striking vertical strings. And whereas the Grand hammer can fall back from the string entirely by gravity, the upright hammer needs to be helped to resume its rest position if it is going to be ready to respond quickly to further striking of the key. Also in most horizontal Grand pianos the hammers lie under the strings and strike upwards. If the instrument is made vertical, the hammers will be behind the strings as the player sees them, and the linkage from the keys to the hammers must pass under the bottom end of the strings. If therefore an upright instrument is made with the strings going down to the floor, the keys can't conveniently be linked to hammers on the other side of the strings, and it becomes necessary to design an action with hammers in front of the strings. This problem was not tackled immediately and the early upright pianos were therefore fairly high. And although they saved a certain amount of room space, they were no cheaper than the horizontal version. It was not until the invention of the square piano that the possibility of an instrument of reasonable size and price was realised.

The first thing to be said about the square piano is

that it isn't square. It is in fact an oblong shape, and from its outside looks very much like a clavichord. It is therefore still a horizontal piano. The earliest known example of the instrument was made in 1742 by a Bavarian, Johann Socher. The action is very basic. There is no escapement, and the hammer is simply flung up against the string by a jack fixed to the end of the key. The key itself is physically stopped before the hammer stroke is completed so there is no danger of the hammer being held pressed against the string by the key: it is free to fall back after the stroke and rests on top of the jack until the key is released, when both jack and hammer revert to their starting position.

The first square piano was introduced into England about 1755, and we have already seen that the arrival of Johann Christoph Zumpe in England in 1760 was

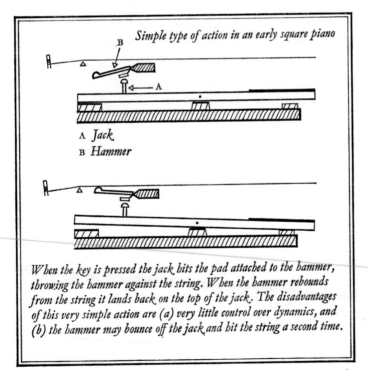

*Simple type of action in an early square piano*

A *Jack*
B *Hammer*

*When the key is pressed the jack hits the pad attached to the hammer, throwing the hammer against the string. When the hammer rebounds from the string it lands back on the top of the jack. The disadvantages of this very simple action are (a) very little control over dynamics, and (b) the hammer may bounce off the jack and hit the string a second time.*

one of the factors that marked the beginning of the great period of English piano-making. Zumpe began making square pianos with the simple sort of action mentioned above, and by 1767 he had left Broadwoods and is recorded as having set up in business on his own in Princess Street, Hanover Square, in London. Zumpe's square pianos were the right instrument at the right time to set in motion the commercial success story of the piano; something new and intriguing, not *too* cheap, but inexpensive enough to attract substantial sales, and with the bonus of having the Queen's music teacher as a supporter. When we talk about the success of a firm like Broadwoods, for example, we have to remember that by far the greater part of their output consisted of square pianos for domestic use, in spite of their insistence that the most fashionable instrument was the Grand. In the 1830s, out of an average of about 1650 pianos made by Broadwoods each year, about 1300 were squares.

But the square piano existed in more sophisticated forms as well. The simple action without any escapement worked adequately within certain limits, but a jack hitting a hammer shank and throwing the hammer against the string doesn't allow for very sensitive control of the blow. On the other hand, if the jack can follow the hammer through almost to the point where the hammer hits the string it will effectively prevent the hammer's return unless there is an escapement. We've seen that the escapement allows the hammer to fall back almost to its rest position *while the key is still pressed down*. It is this escapement principle that enables the player to produce a wide dynamic range by the way he presses the key. So a modified form of Cristofori's 1726 'Double' action with the escapement was applied to the square piano, though the simple or 'Single' action continued to be used as well.

70

Then to meet the extra keyboard range requirements of some of the music at the turn of the century 'additional keys' were fitted to the treble of many instruments. The soundboard of the basic square piano already occupied that area of the inside of the instrument that wasn't taken up by keys and hammers, and at first sight it seemed that to extend the hammers in the treble would mean removing a section of the soundboard, thereby reducing its vibrating area to the detriment of its tone. However in 1794 William Southwell of Dublin had the idea of placing the extra hammers *under* part of the soundboard and cutting a slit in the board just big enough for the hammer heads to pass through. The extra strings of course were placed above the soundboard, and aligned so that their striking point was just above the slit for the hammers.

In many respects the development of the square occurred side by side with that of the Grand. This was especially so in America where public solo piano recitals took much longer to get established (they were rare in the States before about 1870). This may partly explain why the Grand piano was so slow in establishing itself in America: although it had been both imported and made locally in small numbers in the earlier part of the nineteenth century it was not until the 1840s and 1850s that very much attention was given to it. The first one-piece iron frame (see page 93) was fitted to a square piano, not a Grand. And whereas in Europe the decline of the square started before the middle of the nineteenth century, the American version didn't begin to lose popularity until the last quarter of the century. At the end it was given a dramatic send-off. In 1903 the Society of American Piano Manufacturers built a fifty-foot-high pyramid of square pianos and set fire to them.

But in its day the square piano was immensely popular. Mozart fell in love with one of the early instruments, and they found their way into thousands of homes. With their wooden frames, thin strings, and small leather-tipped hammers they have the same sort of bright edgy tone as the corresponding Grands, but a much smaller volume. They can still make delightful domestic instruments, and it is a tragedy that so many have been carelessly and ignorantly destroyed, or had their insides torn out to convert them to furniture.

Still, we have to remember that the domestic piano *is* a piece of furniture, and this factor has always influenced its size, shape, and design. As the square became more sophisticated, so it became bigger. In America it reached enormous proportions – some 7 feet in length. But if more pianos were to be sold they had to be produced in a form that would fit the living-rooms of the less well off, if possible without losing any of the qualities they had already acquired, and still at an attractive price.

As we have seen, the upright Grand didn't really fulfil all these requirements. The answer was first provided, almost simultaneously, by Isaac Hawkins in America and Matthias Müller in Vienna. In 1800 both hit upon the idea of standing the piano on its end, but with the tail at the bottom and actually resting on the floor. The wrest pins are now at the top of the instrument, and the hammers strike from the front. Hawkins' version was particularly remarkable because he suspended his sounding-board in a metal frame and also used a metal wrest-pin block – this eight years before Broadwoods' first tentative use of iron bars to strengthen the treble end of their Grands. These two new upright designs stood about four and a half to five feet in height.

It was to be some years before the upright piano became a viable commercial proposition, and various improvements had to be achieved first. For one thing, Grand pianos up to this time had normally been straight strung – that is, all the strings ran parallel to each other along the length of the instrument. But the strings are shorter in the treble and longer in the bass, and if such an instrument were to be made smaller the string length would have to be shorter. Yet there was a minimum length for the bass strings below which it was very difficult to get a good bass tone.

We can see now that the obvious answer is to cross-string, so that the bass strings are diagonal to the frame and overlap the other strings. This not only makes it possible to keep a reasonable length, but also helps to distribute the string tension more evenly round the frame. For some reason, however, the idea was slow to gain acceptance even though the principle had been used by a pupil of Silbermann's, Christian Ernst Friederici, as early as 1745.

William Southwell, now working in London, produced in 1807 an upright piano with the tail resting on the floor but of Grand dimensions, thus allowing a good bass string length. This was known as the cabinet piano, but at seven or eight feet in height it could not be called a small piano, and it was if anything more expensive than a conventional Grand, and without any musical benefits. Nevertheless, it was made in considerable numbers, notably by Clementi, and was no doubt popular as an imposing piece of furniture.

So attempts to produce an adequate upright piano continued. In 1811 Southwell experimented with a square-piano design placed on its side. The same year Robert Wornum, another English maker, produced a small upright with vertical strings which was called a cottage piano, and he continued improving his design until 1828. The height of this instrument, also known as a pianino, was only 3′ 10″. The design was copied in France, Germany and Austria. But the breakthrough really came, still in 1828, when Henri Pape, who was making cottage pianos based on Wornum's design, introduced the principle of cross-stringing to the upright. It was now possible to produce a reasonably good tone over the whole keyboard range from a small instrument.

The action of the modern upright piano is different from that of the Grand. Although a modification of Erard's repetition action was applied to uprights it was Wornum's 'tape-check action', which he was using in the 1830s, that became the standard, and it is the basis of upright actions today. The principle is that a tape attached to the hammer butt speeds the hammer's return from the string. In this way the hammer is made ready for a further stroke from the key, and a reasonable speed of repetition is possible (see Appendix, pp. 106-7).

Cross-stringing of uprights was introduced in England in 1835 and the following year an English maker in Leeds patented a complete iron frame for the upright. The days of the square piano, in Europe at least, were numbered. By 1850 the upright accounted for close on ninety per cent of English piano production, with Grands providing another five per cent or so. The squares that were still being made were mainly for export.

In spite of the efforts to make the upright smaller many of the Victorian pianos were substantial pieces of furniture. Dark, solid, rectangular objects, with a candle-holder set each side of the player, these were the instruments that provided one of the main sources of home entertainment, at least until the First World War. It is perhaps tempting to over-emphasise the fashionableness of the nineteenth-century piano and to forget the enormous amount of sheer pleasure and fun that was derived from it. Illustrations from the last half of the century show people dancing to the accompaniment of the piano, groups clustered around the piano with violin or voice or whatever instrument was available, young ladies singing at the piano, groups of family and friends listening raptly to young ladies playing the piano, stern fathers standing over their small daughters practising at the piano. Perhaps today we would not regard the quality of much of the playing very highly. But music has always had two quite clearly separated functions, one as worship and then later as secular art, the other simply as entertainment. For all the work that may have been done on the Studies of Cramer, Czerny, or Clementi, for all the efforts to master the sonatas of Beethoven or the waltzes of Chopin or Mendelssohn's *Songs Without Words*, far the greater part of the fun lay in music from the shows, dramatic pieces descriptive of famous battles, heavily sentimental songs, or dance music.

Of course music publishers were quick to seize the opportunities, and countless copies of sheet music poured from the presses. One enterprising man called Harrison as far back as 1797 had begun publishing in weekly instalments a *Pianoforte Magazine* containing pieces suitable for the piano at home. He also offered the extra incentive that, on completing the purchase of all 250 issues at 2s. 6d. a time, the buyer could claim a brand-new pianoforte said to be worth at least twenty-five guineas.

Much of the music played during the nineteenth century was no doubt very bad by 'Art' standards;

certainly much of it was cast in well-established and oft-repeated formulas which would make it both immediately familiar to the ear and relatively easy to play. But when one witnesses the sagging jaws and the glazed eyes in front of the tv set today the communal making of even bad music seems a refreshingly creative activity by comparison.

In the period from 1850 to 1910 the annual rate of piano manufacture in Britain went up from 25,000 to 75,000. In America, over the same period, the output rose from about 9000 to a staggering 360,000 pianos each year, putting her unchallengeably into the leadership of world piano-production. One factor that contributed to this enormous rise in America was the lowering of prices brought about by intensified factory methods. Well before 1900 the making of individual parts of pianos had become the specialist responsibility of separate firms. This reached the point where the function of many piano-making firms was reduced to that of buying the parts and assembling the instruments, perhaps with some individual characteristics in the casework or finish, and their own name on the keyboard lid. Some went even further and sent pianos out with no name, leaving the retailer to add whatever name he thought would make the best impression. Indeed, some names on these pianos came perilously close to those of distinguished piano-making firms. The name 'Steinmay' on a piano could lead a not too knowledgeable buyer to believe he was getting an instrument of repute.

As far back as 1880 Steinways were claiming that they were the only makers in America whose pianos were entirely their own. The same is largely true today of quality pianos – Grands and the more expensive uprights – though a number of parts are now produced by separate firms. Steinways, for example, do not cast their own frames, and some parts of the action are made by specialist firms. But everything is still made to Steinways' own design and is exclusive to their pianos.

During the present century the domestic piano has been threatened by the changing pattern of home life. In the inter-war years the focus of entertainment was tending to move away from the home, with cinemas and dance halls providing new and exciting ways of spending the evenings. At the same time the radio and gramophone were giving access to good performances of music of all sorts, including piano music, to a rapidly expanding proportion of the population. In due course, and pre-dictably, the piano industry felt the pinch. The 1910 piano output of 75,000 became 67,000 in 1930 and 38,000 in 1939. During the Second World War pro-duction ceased altogether, but since that time the numbers have never approached even the 1939 figure. In 1965 the British piano industry made only 13,000 pianos.

By this time television had taken over from the cinema, and the focus of entertainment was returning to the home, though in a much more passive sense than before. This was surely the end of the domestic piano. But against all predictions the sale of pianos and the number of people learning to play has again been increasing. In 1972 20,000 pianos were made, half of which were sold at home – and a growing number of pupils sit the Associated Board exams. This tendency is hard to account for, since it really cannot be explained any more in terms of impressing the neighbours. The new domestic status symbols are the colour tv and the hi-fi. Can it be that today people simply want to *play*

77

the piano, even though they have ringing in their ears by means of at least two loudspeakers, stunning technical performances by a plethora of brilliant pianists?

In fact the evidence about today's domestic pianos is itself confusing. There are some two and a quarter million households in Britain with pianos, but a survey carried out in 1972 for the Piano Publicity Association shows that a large proportion of privately owned pianos have not been tuned for at least two years. (The proportion varies, using the survey's own categories, from thirty-five per cent of upper and middle-class owners to eighty-two per cent of semi-skilled and unskilled manual workers and State pensioners with no other income.) Whether this means that these pianos are unplayed, or that the pianists don't notice their instruments are out of tune is impossible to say, but the survey does show that in almost a fifth of all households owning a piano no one plays it.

On the other hand, there are 2,630,000 people living in houses with pianos who can play to some extent, and there must presumably be a sizeable number of pianists in households without pianos. Piano-owning families are still predominantly middle class, and about two-thirds of the pianists are female. One other interesting fact emerging from the survey is that ownership of pianos is markedly higher in rural areas – twenty-two per cent of homes in Wales, for example, and twenty per cent in the north of England compared with only six per cent in London and five per cent in eastern England. Perhaps this is partly accounted for by greater domestic mobility in the south-east and a correspondingly lesser likelihood that the old parlour piano would still be in the family. But could it also mean that in areas where the town goes dead at 10 o'clock in the evening people are more likely to be thrown back on their own resources for entertainment – that they are actually more likely to *play* the piano?

It would need another survey to find out what sort of music people are playing today, and it is difficult to arrive at accurate figures for the sale of piano music. But it seems that nearly half of it is pop music, and about another third consists of light music other than pop. This still leaves fifteen to twenty per cent for the classics, and as might be expected the familiar names, Beethoven, Mozart, Chopin, top the list.

The buying of a piano is a bigger undertaking than most people realise. In the first place potential buyers usually have no idea of the price. The P.P.A. survey shows that people thinking of buying only expect to pay up to a maximum of £300; yet the *cheapest* English-made upright today costs about £350 and a fine German upright can cost £1400.[1] But, apart from cost considerations, how do you choose a piano? Often people run their fingers over the most expensive instrument, which has probably been placed in the most eye-catching position in the showroom, and then hope to find *that* quality in a piano at a tenth of the price. But the problem can be even greater because the majority of buyers are looking for a piano for their children, and very probably can't play themselves at all. They are therefore entirely dependent on the salesman's demonstration of piano-tone.

Pianos today can be broadly divided into two categories – bright-toned and soft-toned – but within each category there is quite a variety of tone qualities available. In the past people have tended to want a softer

[1] The general trend of price increases and the introduction of Value Added Tax have substantially raised prices recently. A German-made Grand that cost £2800 in January 1973 was priced at £3400 in July of the same year.

tone from an upright than from a Grand but there has
been some movement over the past thirty years towards
a more brilliant sound. The best way to assess the
different tone qualities is to make sure that the same
piece of music is played on each piano being tried. If
the player, or the salesman, chooses a different piece
for each piano to underline the best qualities of that
instrument, then comparison becomes impossible.

The greater demand today is for small upright pianos,
and their appearance as pieces of furniture is an important factor – they must fit in with the rest of the room.
Indeed, some people are still prepared to buy pianos
as desirable furniture rather than as musical instruments. (One London store recently sold an upright
piano to a household where no one had any intention
of playing it, but the chosen instrument had to be the
best in the showroom – at £1400.)

The British piano industry today is still very much
a family affair, unlike that in America where the massive
mergers which took place early in the present century
swallowed up most of the family names. English uprights have their frames cast by independent foundries
and some makers buy their piano actions from specialist
firms. But in general the English pianos available today
are not mass-produced and the selling price will usually
reflect the quality. A number of very good Japanese
uprights are available in the middle-quality range today, though they are not likely to be any cheaper than
English pianos of comparable quality.

Although the piano was particularly suited to the
factory process in John Broadwood's day, it is really
less suited to the highly mechanised and automated
production methods available today. There is still
craftsmanship involved in making modern upright
pianos, and a large part of the cost of a piano pays for

*Two thrones, c.* 1880. *Cartoon by Du Maurier.*

*Steinway Large Square Piano,* 1872. *See page* 72.

*Lyre-shaped Piano by J. C. Schleip, c. 18*
*See page 90.*

*Steinway-Welte Reproducing Piano, c. 1910.*
*See page 87.*

this craftsmanship. It is questionable whether there is any more a need for several different firms producing very much the same kind of instrument, but it may be that the spirit of craft is better maintained in smaller units even if on simple economic grounds they make less sense.

For the future, there is little development in either construction or tone-quality envisaged. Resin glues and modern methods of drying wood have made possible the use of multiple laminated timber for piano cases, wrest planks, and even for the soundboard itself. This has improved the durability of the whole structure and made it less susceptible to climatic changes and the effects of central heating. There are many moving parts on a piano, and these are obviously prone to wear out, as are the felt pads on the hammers which have to take quite a beating from being repeatedly hurled against the strings. Attempts have been made to use plastic in some of the moving parts, but these have not proved very successful.

Many of the upright pianos made today find their way into schools, and perhaps it is here that one of the big hopes for the future of the domestic instrument lies. There are few people who don't respond to music in some degree, but the day has not yet come when it is taken really seriously as an important element in every child's life. If music became a full member of the school curriculum, and if every child had the opportunity of learning to play the piano at school, perhaps the upright could become as much a part of the domestic furniture as the television set – and as much used.

*View of John Brinsmead and Sons Pianoforte works, London NW, 1883.*

# 8
# Oddities

From Cristofori's first practical instrument in 1709 through to the fine, powerful mid-nineteenth-century instruments like the Erard of 1868, the piano's history is a story of continuing and accelerating progress. But along the way there have been some unusual, even bizarre, digressions. Ingenious minds have seen in the piano enormous scope for their inventive talents. Yet the piano has mostly resisted these attempts to divert it from its course, even though some of the ideas that were generated and given practical form had some good sense in them.

Take the keyboard, for example. Since our hands move around roughly in an arc from our body, what could be more sensible than to make the keyboard also in an arc, so that all the notes could be reached with equal ease? This was tried in 1824 in Vienna, and other attempts have been made since then, but it never caught on and nothing is heard of it now. On the present keyboard, too, the width of the keys is designed for an adult hand, and small children therefore cannot stretch the same number of notes, whereas violins are now made in such small sizes that children under two can learn to play. A lady in Paris in the nineteenth century invented a keyboard with narrower keys which could be placed on top of the regular keyboard. Today we don't apparently think this is necessary and miniature pianists have to wait until they grow to the right size.

Perhaps the greatest fault in the design of the keyboard we now have is that the arrangement of black and white notes means that each of the twelve major scales has to be played with a different positioning of the fingers. Nowadays we take this for granted, but to anyone discovering the modern keyboard for the first time it would seem a ludicrous arrangement. Yet here again the piano keyboards that have been invented from 1811 onwards to enable all twelve scales to be played with the same fingering have not caught on. One disadvantage of such inventions is that there would have to be a major relearning of piano technique if they were ever to become more than an occasional oddity. Transposing pianos have been made, in which by moving the keyboard, or some other parts of the instrument, the same keys can be made to sound different notes. For example, a piece in B major or C sharp major could be made to sound at the right pitch while the pianist was actually playing the keys of C major. This would have had particular value in the days before a standard pitch had been agreed (see Chapter 4) when a pianist might find himself with a woodwind player whose middle C was at a different pitch. It could be useful too in transposing songs if the written key is out of the singer's range. A transposing square piano made by Broadwoods in 1801 still exists, but today the ability to transpose at sight is regarded as a valuable skill in a pianist.

There have been many attempts to increase the scope of the piano as a musical instrument and these attempts have taken a number of different forms. First there are those which simply expand on the basic piano idea – the Duoclave, for example. This consisted of two pianos built into the same case, and was intended, obviously, for two players at the same time. In one of its versions, the double Grand, it took the form of a long rectangular box with a keyboard at each end. Inside there are really two separate Grand pianos, their curves neatly fitted together. The piano has also been combined with the harpsichord in this way, and there are other examples of piano and harpsichord actions built into a single instrument with one keyboard only. Piano and organ have also been combined, producing what was known as an 'organised' piano. Octave coupling has also been introduced to the piano, enabling the player to produce octaves while only playing single notes.

The nineteenth century saw a number of attempts to increase the sustaining capacity of the piano. Some of these still use the basic piano principle, like the repeating hammer action. A patent was taken out by Isaac Hawkins in 1800 for a system to make the hammer repeatedly hit the string for as long as the key was pressed down. Other attempts departed from the piano principle. In one case the strings were set in vibration by a sort of circular bow, and in another currents of air were used to make them sound.

One of the more substantial episodes in the piano's history, but still outside the main path of its development, concerned the production of a whole range of other sounds and effects from the one instrument. For a time the piano became almost a small orchestra on its own. It's easy to see the attraction of this idea when one considers the sort of dramatic programme music that was so popular in the earlier part of the nineteenth century. These instruments had an array of pedals, and so long as you managed to press the right one you could produce the bassoon effect, caused by a strip of parchment touching the vibrating strings, or the cymbal effect, when brass strips are struck against the bass strings. A drum could be made to sound by arranging for a parchment drum head, or the soundboard of the piano, to be hit by a stick. A triangle sound could be simulated, using small bells, and various sorts of lute or harp effects were possible using strips of cloth or leather on the strings.

Some of these effects were particularly prompted by a craze for Turkish music which grew up in the last half of the eighteenth century. The introduction of Turkish instruments – various drums, cymbals and triangles – to the military band prompted composers like Mozart and Beethoven to incorporate these Turkish characteristics into some of their music. (Reference has already been made to the well-known last movement of Mozart's Piano Sonata in A, K331, the 'Rondo alla Turca', which can well be played with some of the effects referred to above.)

All these innovations have long since been abandoned and we are left with only some surviving instruments to remind us of what they were like. These pianos with effects have often been scorned as 'unmusical' but at least they had to be worked by human beings. During the present century, since the modern piano has been with us, a much greater threat emerged.

The idea of mechanically operated keyboard instruments had been in the air a long time before 1900. The barrel organ, in which the air flow to individual organ pipes is controlled by metal pins set in a revolving cylinder (or barrel) opening and closing valves, had been around since the fifteenth century. In 1825 the Clementi piano firm applied the principle to the piano, so that the turning of the cylinder was made to control the hammers striking the keys.

In France in about 1863 a machine was made which could automatically operate the keys of a normal piano. This machine was activated by air pressure, and it was a device of this sort that was patented by E. S. Votey in 1897 in America as the Pianola. It rapidly became the rage, and by 1919 the player-piano, as it was sometimes known, accounted for more than half of the entire piano output of the USA. The pianola works by means of a long roll of strong paper with perforations punched in it. Each perforation represents a note, and the length of the perforation corresponds to the length of time the note should sound. The paper roll passes over a row of air jets, each corresponding to one note of the piano. As a perforation in the paper passes over a jet, the released air pressure activates the hammer for that note. So a whole Beethoven sonata or musical number from a show can be translated into a perforated roll of paper and then reproduced on the piano. All the player has to do is pedal with his feet to provide both the air pressure to operate the hammers, and the power to transport the paper roll across the air jets.

In time this mechanism was built *into* the piano and by the use of various levers it became possible to control the speed and dynamics of the music. With the more advanced machines the control of expression could be quite subtle. It also became possible, with the Reproducing Piano, to 'record' actual performances by great pianists. They would play on a specially adapted piano and the movement of their fingers on the keys would cause a piano roll to be marked. These marks would then be made into perforations. Many great pianists made piano rolls, including Paderewski, Artur Rubinstein and Moiseiwitsch. Composers, too, like Grieg, Debussy and Ravel, performed their own music for the Reproducing Piano.

The player-pianos were marvellous machines and are now becoming collectors' pieces. They were made

87

both as Grands and uprights, and Steinways produced their own Grand version, called Steinway – Duo – Art. But perhaps it's as well that their vogue was short-lived. If you have a machine in the house that can play your own piano much better than you can, there would seem to be little incentive to learn to play it at all. Or is that too pessimistic? Would the individual's need to express himself still have won in the end?

Anyway, the gramophone and the radio made short work of the player-piano. They had all the advantages: they were cheaper and smaller; more music became available on records than on piano rolls; and with the radio you didn't need records at all. Although the best player-pianos could give good quality repro-duction the majority couldn't compete with the quality of *performance* available from the new media. So, although in the early 1920s the player-pianos were at the height of their popularity in Britain and Europe as well as in America, by the end of the decade they were practically obsolete.

Today the piano is about as functional as it can get. It *looks* like a piano, and it doesn't claim to be anything more. Even the candle-holders, which clung on for years after people stopped using candles, have now been removed. This all makes good sense on economic grounds. The piano already costs a lot more than most people expect to pay, and since we don't identify ourselves with our pianos in the same way we do with our cars, there is not much commercial pressure to build pianos with exciting visual features.

Piano-makers didn't always feel the need for such conformity. Many of the old pianos and fortepianos surviving today are truly beautiful pieces of work. Even the simple instruments are often *elegantly* simple, and some are anything but simple. Broadwoods, in

*Top: Upright Grand Piano*
*by Clementi, c. 1815. See page 89.*

*Below: Elegant Square Piano, c. 1812 by Tomkison.*

*Babcock Square Piano with cast-iron frame. See page 93.*

*First Steinway factory in New York, 1853.*

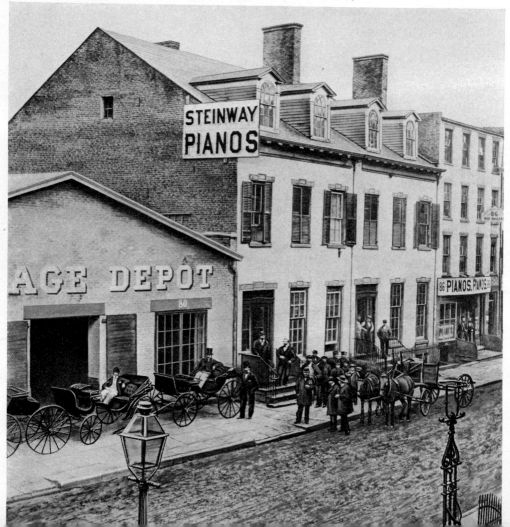

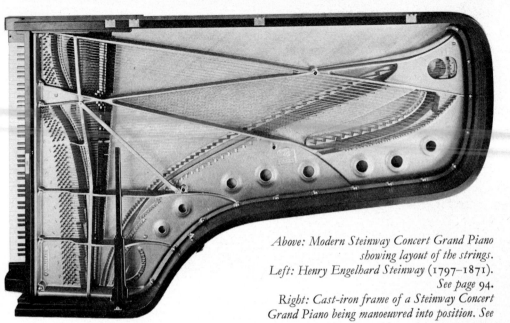

*Above: Modern Steinway Concert Grand Piano showing layout of the strings.*
*Left: Henry Engelhard Steinway (1797–1871). See page 94.*
*Right: Cast-iron frame of a Steinway Concert Grand Piano being manoeuvred into position. See page 97.*

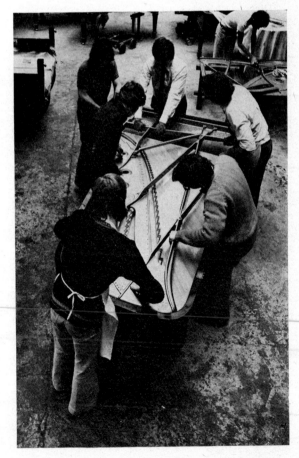

*Above: Action of a modern Steinway Grand Piano.*

*Below: Detail of a modern Steinway Grand Piano action. See diagrams on pages 108 and 109.*

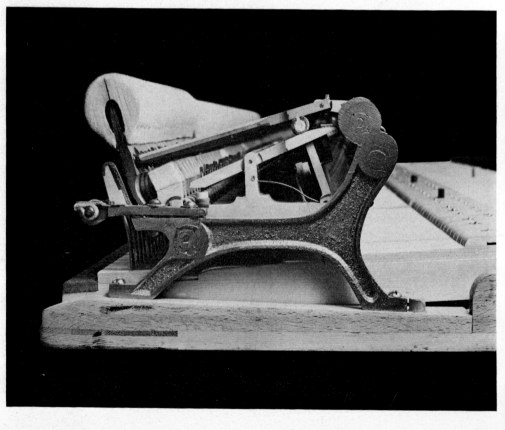

1796, made a piano for Don Manuel de Godoy, who intended it as a gift for the Queen of Spain. The case-work was designed by Sheraton, and is of satinwood inlaid with various other woods and decorated with Wedgwood and Tassie medallions. It is a mere detail, in such a superbly decorated piano, that Sheraton omitted to include any pedals in his design.

But some of the most impressive instruments, to the eyes of a non-specialist, are those which look least like our modern idea of a piano. The square piano itself is a case in point. With its lid closed it resembles more a table, and some of these instruments are very elegant pieces of furniture indeed. They have as much care lavished on their decoration as if their whole function was to be decorative. Some of them have little drawers and could obviously double as writing tables. There are also pianos whose dual role is more blatant. Friederici, who was one of the first to attempt an upright piano, later made one in the form of a chest of drawers. Another instrument, which must surely be unique, had a bed built into its base. This bed could be pulled out when required, and on either side of it were two cupboards, one for bed clothes, the other providing space for a wash-basin, jug and towel.

In many other instances the requirements of the actual piano design have led makers to build extra-ordinary cases for their instruments. In some upright Grands, for example, where the broad end of the piano rests at keyboard level and the tail end sticks in the air, the upper part has been enclosed in a rectangular outer case fitted with doors, the extra space between the narrow tail of the piano and the side of the outer case containing shelves for books or ornaments.

Another interesting form of the instrument is the Giraffe piano. This also is an upright Grand with its tail in the air, but with the broad end resting on the ground. The shape of the tail, far from being concealed in a rectangular case, is often elaborated by means of a design such as a scroll at the top. One such instrument made in about 1810 by a Dutchman, Van der Hoef, is now in the Victoria and Albert Museum. It also has pedals for the Turkish effects, and it was featured in two paintings by Sir William Orchardson. In one, entitled 'Music, when soft voices die, vibrates in the memory', a young lady sits at the piano, in a large elegant room, languorously turning the pages of a piece of music. In the other, 'The Lyric', she sits looking wistfully towards the painter, her pen poised over a piece of paper in her lap.

Other pianos came in other shapes, some lyre, some pyramid, determined to greater or lesser extent by the pattern of their stringing. All these instruments clearly had one common aim – to be seen as well as heard. They couldn't be made like that today, they are not of our age. The piano is probably the most expensive single item of furniture in our homes, but we no longer want it to make an exhibition of itself.

# 9
# The Modern Piano

If a piano like the Erard of 1868 (see p. 66) is symbolic of the modern sound it is in some respects still quite a way from what we regard as beautiful tone today. By describing it as a modern sound we have to use as a yardstick what is accepted as good quality at the present time. Whether that particular quality is good for all types and periods of piano music is a separate argument that is dealt with elsewhere. The fact is that within fairly narrow limits there is now a consensus of opinion as to what constitutes good piano sound.

The change of yardstick from that of the old forte-pianos puts the Erard at a certain disadvantage. The argument has already been put that the earlier pianos should be regarded not as inferior versions of a modern instrument but rather as instruments making a notably different sound with qualities all their own. And it's a pity that we can't listen to this Erard with 1868 ears. In its time it must have seemed a truly magnificent instrument, and it is not really fair to judge it with hindsight. But today it cannot escape comparison with modern pianos, and in that context it must appear less successful, however interesting and enjoyable it is to listen to as a historical instrument. For one thing it is not as resonant a piano, especially at the extreme ends of its range. Its tone is not as full or as mellow or as liquid (we all have our own words to describe piano sound) as a modern Grand. It still has a trace of the 'jangly' quality of the wood-framed pianos, but without quite their delicacy or charm. This is an instrument that is seriously striving to be big.

In fact, in spite of all that had been achieved up to the middle of the nineteenth century there were still some major developments to come, and for the first of these the scene changes once again, this time to America. It's not known exactly when the first piano was heard there, but it begins to be heard *of* in the 1770s when a few English-made instruments were finding their way across the Atlantic. It was not long before home-produced examples were being made, but the London fortepiano was the model on which the early American industry was based. Even so the American copies were not thought to have the same class as their English originals. Oddly enough it was Clementis which became the most respected import; Broadwoods were less successful, perhaps partly because the financial terms they offered to importers were not sufficiently attractive.

The same incentives to strengthen the frame of the piano in Britain and Europe – increased keyboard range, raising of the pitch, the demand for a greater dynamic range, and the consequent increase in string tension – of course affected the American product as well, but there was an additional factor of a more immediately practical nature. The extremes of climate to be found in the United States made it even more difficult to keep an instrument in tune, and at the same time subjected the wooden frame to damaging stresses. Perhaps the new adventurous spirit in the States was prepared to take risks and try out new ideas at a time when the European piano industry was firmly established and inclined to settle into a traditionalist frame of mind. At all events, the next major development – the final link, as it were, that made possible the growth of the powerful sonorous instrument of today – was the responsibility of an American.

We have already seen how in Philadelphia in 1800 the Englishman Hawkins made an upright piano with a large amount of metal in the frame. Twenty-five years later, in 1825, at the time when Beethoven had just received his Graf fortepiano with an all-wood frame, Alpheus Babcock of Boston took the revolutionary step of casting the whole frame of a square piano in one solid piece of iron. Now at last the ground was laid for a really strong, stable and climate-resistant piano.

Babcock was more piano-maker than businessman, and it was left to others to exploit the idea fully. His partner of a few years, John Mackay, split up from him and in due course took his money and his business talents to another young piano-maker in Boston, Jonas Chickering. Chickering took up the idea of the one-piece iron frame, and it was he who in the 1840s applied it to the Grand piano, which as we have seen was comparatively unknown in America at this time. In New York the idea of the cast-iron frame was slower in catching on, but there is no doubt that Chickering's acceptance of the principle was a major factor in establishing the firm of Chickering and Mackay as the foremost piano-makers in the country. By the mid-nineteenth century they were making more pianos than any other American manufacturer – about a thousand a year – though it's worth remembering that Broadwoods were producing 1500 to 2000 a year as far back as 1810. So by 1850 the American piano industry had captured the local market and the import of English pianos into America, having been on the decline for some twenty years, had virtually ceased. In that same year there arrived in America a man whose name has been identified ever since with the making of the finest pianos, Henry Steinway.

Amongst the immigrants to America in the last twenty years of the eighteenth century had been a number of German musicians and instrument-makers. Once again we see the influence of German piano-makers being spread abroad. The flow from Germany steadily increased during the next century and reached enormous proportions in the 1840s and 1850s. Their impact on the American musical scene was of major importance. They brought with them their concept of music as 'Art', and of course they also brought with them the music of Beethoven, Mozart, Schubert, Schumann and Mendelssohn, and they established a supremacy in music-making which can still be recognised in the names of countless musicians in America today.

Amongst these new arrivals in 1850 was Heinrich Steinweg, whose son Karl had arrived two years earlier to test the temperature of the American piano business. Steinweg was a piano-maker from Braunschweig who was encouraged to look for new territory, as had so many before him, by unsettled conditions at home. Within three years of arriving he had altered his name and the firm of Henry Steinway and Sons had been founded.

Their grasp of the new possibilities that were opening up was immediate and decisive and, for the other American firms then operating, catastrophic. Two years after establishing their business they won the first award against all competition, and by unanimous judgement, at a Trade Fair in New York. That was in 1855. It took them a mere fourteen years more to oust Chickering as the major piano-producing firm in the United States. How was it done? What was the secret of this dramatic success story? First of all they accepted the principle of the complete cast-iron frame from the beginning. The square piano with which the New York award was won had an iron frame. It was also cross-strung – not a new practice since it had been tried in the eighteenth century and was normal in upright pianos after about 1828, but Steinways' approach was more far-reaching. We have already seen that the basic idea of cross-stringing enables better bass tone to be preserved in smaller instruments. Steinways realised that they could make use of this departure from parallel stringing to adjust the spacing of the strings on the bridge, and the position of the bridge itself, so as to make the best possible use of the vibrating areas of the soundboard.

In 1859, four years after their New York Trade Fair success, Steinways were applying their method of cross-stringing to the Grand piano, and from then on increasingly gave their attention to the Grand in place of the more customary large square pianos. In 1865 another Steinway son, Theodore, came over from Germany and brought with him a more exact scientific approach to the production of piano tone. He had studied physics and knew the famous nineteenth-century physicist and acoustician Hermann Helmholtz, who in 1862 had published a major work dealing with the physical characteristics of sound. Thus a more informed attitude could be brought to the problems of vibrating strings and sounding-boards, and what is known as the harmonic content, or the overtones, of individual sounds which determine their tone quality.

An idea originated by Clementi and Co. that Steinways introduced to their pianos was to make use of the section of string between the bridge and the hitch-pin as vibrating material, instead of dampening it with a strip of felt as had previously been done. The treble end of a piano is always a difficult part to make sufficiently resonant, and by fitting another bridge near the hitchpin and calculating the length of this extra bit of string to match that part hit by the hammer it could be made to vibrate 'in sympathy' with it, and thereby enhance the vibrations. Steinways also brought more precise calculations to deciding where, along the length of the string, the hammer should strike. The vibration of a string is a complex matter, and the way it vibrates can be influenced not only by the quality of the hammer head and the force of the blow, but also by the exact point on the string where the blow takes place. Broadwoods had first taken scientific advice to determine the striking point as far back as 1788. Steinways were now able to predict much more accurately what tone quality would be produced.

Steinway Grand pianos came to be increasingly used on the concert stage, and piano manufacturers fought for the patronage of the great concert artists. In due course Steinways secured such legendary names as Anton Rubinstein in 1872 and Paderewski in 1891, and while letters of recommendation were sometimes given rather indiscriminately, the acid test was whether *your* piano was played. The battles for patronage were sometimes rough, but by the time of the Paris Exposition of 1867 Steinways were already in a position of formidable strength. Their pianos astounded the world, and the great names of old – Broadwood, Pleyel, Erard – were effectively out of the race. Steinways' great American rival, Chickering, signed up Hans von Bülow for a concert tour in 1872, but there were various disagreements and the tour was not a great success. The firm went into a long decline, and virtually disappeared in the early years of this century.

Meanwhile new life was stirring in Germany. Two new piano-makers had started up in the 1850s, Julius Blüthner in Leipzig and Carl Bechstein in Berlin. It would be difficult to say at what point they decided to follow the same principles of piano design that were being established in America, but as the main European contenders along with the older firm of Bösendorfer for the world market in concert quality Grand pianos it is true to say that their differences from Steinway principles lie in detail rather than in fundamental concept. Blüthners used a different action, the Blüthner single action, up to 1925, but since then their design has been based on the Schwander action, derived from Erard's repetition action and now in general use for Grand pianos.

Steinway opened a London distribution centre in 1877, and three years later built a factory in Hamburg where Steinway pianos are made to this day. Almost all Steinways used in Britain are made in Hamburg. In 1890 came the accolade of a Royal Warrant. By the turn of the century the modern piano that we know today had been established.

What is this modern Grand piano really like inside? The rather bulky curved shape of its case is basically determined by the contours of the solid cast-iron frame. This seems a massive piece of metal when you compare it with the slender elegant lines of the early fortepiano, but the total string tension has risen from two and a half to three tons on a fortepiano of about 1800 to something like thirty tons on today's Concert Grand. Small wonder that it takes four or five men to manoeuvre the modern Grand piano frame into the case.

This increase of tension is only possible because of the iron frame. The hitchpins are now cast as part of the frame, so there is no possibility of their moving. The treble strings, three to each note, can be made longer because the frame can stand the extra tension needed to keep the same pitch. These longer strings can vibrate more freely, quite apart from the extra length that vibrates in sympathy. In the bass, where there are two strings to each note (except for the bottom few where there is only one), the strings can be made thicker to accept the heavier hammer blow of the modern piano and give more resonance. They are now made of steel with one or two windings of copper to give them greater mass. And here again the frame can stand the extra tension needed to produce the same pitch from the heavier strings.

A heavier blow needs a bigger hammer and the felt of the modern hammer bears little relation to the little leather tips of the early hammers. They have a thick, rounded covering in the bass and a thinner more pointed tip in the treble. These strings and hammers have to be of sufficient strength to withstand very considerable force, but they also have to respond to the most delicate touch with equal reliability, and it is the piano action that converts the energy from the

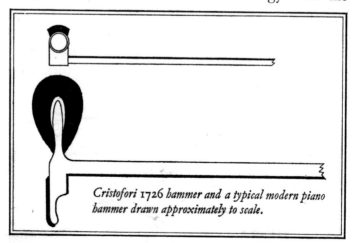

*Cristofori 1726 hammer and a typical modern piano hammer drawn approximately to scale.*

pianist's fingers into the musical vibration of the strings. The modern piano action is a wonderful mechanism, intricate in operation for what might at first seem a simple mechanical function, but sensitive to an incredibly wide range of dynamic control. The many refinements in its design have produced a mechanism which aims to allow maximum responsiveness for minimum expenditure of effort. The merest stroke can produce a sound of haunting subtlety, while a powerful controlled blow can produce tones of glorious richness that set the adrenalin flowing.

All Grand pianos are now fitted with a basic two pedals, one to raise all the dampers at once leaving all the strings free to vibrate whether struck or not; and the other to shift the whole keyboard and action a little to one side so that the hammers will only strike two strings out of three (or in the bass only one string out of two). This also enables a softer part of the hammer to strike the strings, so that the whole piano tone is softened. Some makers, notably Steinways, provide a third pedal in between the other two. This enables the dampers of selected notes only to be kept off the strings, while the others function normally. If a player presses this pedal while holding down a chord, the dampers of the strings of that chord will be held off but any note played *while* the pedal is pressed down will be damped as usual as soon as that key is released. This third pedal, known as the 'sostenuto', obviously has certain practical benefits but composers have made surprisingly little use of it.

There are many factors that go to make up the quality of sound of a modern piano and its responsiveness to the player: the quality of wood of the soundboard; the design and positioning of the bridge; the strings – the quality of their metal, their size and weight,

99

and their distribution over the soundboard; the point in the scale at which the single and two string notes of the bass give way to the three strings of the middle and treble; and the whole grading of string size so that there is no discernible unevenness of tone as one progresses up the keyboard; the hammers – their weight, the quality, thickness and texture of the felt and its distribution over the keyboard range, the springiness of the hammer shank, and the point at which the hammer strikes the string; the action – its ease and evenness of operation; the keyboard – the weight required to press each key down, and the overall evenness and regulation of the whole mechanism.

Although there is today a recognisable 'modern' piano sound, there are still marginal differences within it. American-built pianos, such as the Baldwin, the Heintzman or the American Steinway, are noticeably brighter than most European instruments. The Japanese Kawai and Yamaha, now available in Europe and extensively used in America, resemble the American. With age they sometimes become bright to the point of harshness. French pianos such as the Gaveau or Pleyel, whilst also bright, are different in quality: they seem less potent. The roundest sound has always come from German pianos, the Hamburg Steinway and Berlin Bechstein in particular, though in recent years Bösendorfers have become considerably brighter.

Obviously there can be considerable variations within any one make. So much depends on the conditions of any particular instrument's hammers, which can now easily be treated to give either rounder or brighter tone, and the making of fine pianos is still a craft with all the attendant risks that craft implies. Apparently identical pianos from the same firm will have their own individual qualities, and many concert artists will specify not only the make of piano they wish to play at a concert but the actual instrument by serial number. They may also vary their choice according to the music they are going to play.

In general the concert piano-makers of today agree that there have been no significant changes in the basic tonal capacities of their pianos this century, although there has been a tendency towards a brighter tone in recent years. But this is more a matter of adjustment within known limits than one of fundamental design. It is also clear that no spectacular developments are foreseen for the future. Improvements in the mechanics – the durability of the moving parts of the action, for example – can be hoped for, but there is no sign of any major new breakthrough. We are all, it seems, broadly happy with what we've got. But is this a happy state of affairs, or does it give cause for worry? After all, it could be argued, the violin has been basically unchanged for some 300 years, and for the most part the instruments of the modern orchestra have stabilised into an acceptable state of design. There is no serious competitor for the piano – the electric piano, the electronic organs of one sort or another, these things have their vogue and their functions, but they have not affected the piano's status or popularity. The keyboard-operated synthesiser is the new thing of the moment, but it's too early to say what will happen to that. The urge to spell out one's personal poetry is one that only the piano has so far been able to satisfy on a really large scale. Production of instruments is rising again, as is the number of people taking piano lessons. The world is overstocked with aspiring concert pianists of astonishing technical skill.

Yet the history of the piano has been part of the history of piano music. If the piano has come to a stop what is going to happen to its music? The twentieth-century piano has, in a sense, got out of step with the composers writing for it. Some of the finest mellow-sounding pianos were built at the height of the output of the percussive, dissonant composers such as Bartók, Prokofiev and Stravinsky. It can be very hard work playing something like the Bartók Sonata (1926) on a Steinway with 'beautiful' tone.

Recently the piano has been asked to fulfil a more difficult role. It is arguable that works like Stockhausen's 'Klavierstücke' or Boulez' 'Structures' don't use the piano to good advantage. Despite all the attempts in these pieces to organise and grade the timbre and dynamics of individual notes, the results do not seem to come across half as effectively as when this technique is applied to a group of tuned percussion instruments. The timbre of the individual notes on the piano is after all only marginally variable. It looks as if this idiom is not the future of the piano. The most colourful and possibly the most significant twentieth-century contribution to the piano's literature is surely Olivier Messiaen's. In works like 'Vingt Regards sur l'Enfant-Jésus', 'Visions de l'Amen' and the extensive 'Catalogue des Oiseaux' he has evolved a new idiom that nevertheless exploits the effects of resonance and timbre at which the piano excels. They are unfortunately appallingly difficult works to learn (and in some cases to play!) but recently more and more pianists have mastered them and we can now hear them both on records and in the concert hall.

Still other composers have sought to find quite different ways of using the existing piano, by using parts of the case or frame or strings with direct percussive blows, by plucking or scraping the strings, by treating the sound produced with electronic apparatus, and a variety of other tricks that do more or less damage to the instrument. Indeed in one celebrated case piano and player have been used as a focal point for four minutes and thirty-three seconds of silence. Some of the results of these ideas are interesting and effective, but the greater part of the concert audience is unmoved, unless to ridicule. It is still to the composers of the past, from Mozart through to Debussy and Ravel, that the piano worshippers flock.

Perhaps this present state of affairs partly explains the ever-growing interest in music of the past. The rediscovery of old works and their performance in more or less authentic manner form a substantial part of today's music activities, and this brings us face to face with the question of the use of original instruments for performing music of earlier centuries. Of course we can never hope to hear the fortepianos of the eighteenth and early nineteenth centuries as they sounded at the time. Our ears, our whole personal aural memories, have been conditioned by years of modern piano, not to mention electronic sounds. And aeroplanes, diesel engines, road drills, and all the other noises of our modern civilisation have accustomed us to a much higher normal level of sound.

Then the actual performance in authentic style is a problem, because although there are a few good forte-pianos available they are still scarce. And when it comes to the performance of concertos the difficulties multiply, because the string and wind instruments of today are different in terms of pitch and design from their eighteenth- and early nineteenth-century ancestors. Few players have, and can play, the early wind instruments, and few violinists will restring and retune their violins for occasional performances.

On the positive side the recent trend towards building recital halls has produced a number of buildings with ideal acoustics not only for solo piano, but also solo harpsichord and solo fortepiano. There have been examples recently of recitals using both fortepiano and modern piano, and there is really no reason why recitals involving these two and the harpsichord should not become quite common, instead of the present assumption that piano music of all periods can only be adequately presented on a modern concert Grand. New harpsichords are today readily available in the form of copies of fine original instruments. Perhaps makers can now turn their attention to producing equally good copies of the early fortepianos. For in spite of the obstacles that stand in the way, it is worth saying again that to hear Haydn and Mozart and Beethoven on instruments of their period is a revelation. Magnificent as the modern piano is for most music of the past 120 years, there is a charm and refinement about the sound of the early fortepianos that amply repays the efforts of listening to them unhampered by our modern concept of good piano sound.

# Appendices

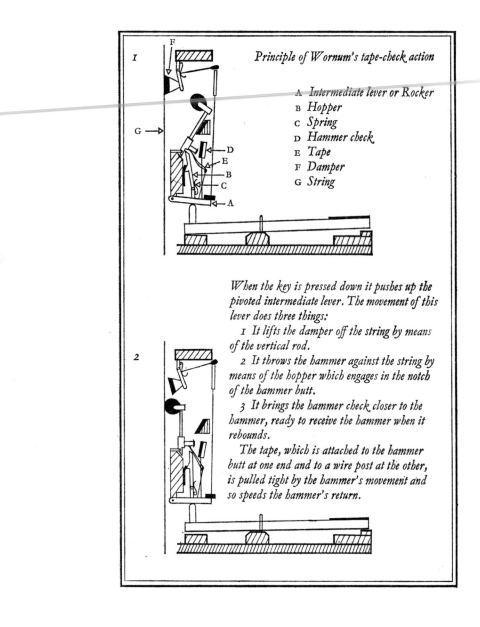

*Principle of Wornum's tape-check action*

A *Intermediate lever or Rocker*
B *Hopper*
C *Spring*
D *Hammer check*
E *Tape*
F *Damper*
G *String*

*When the key is pressed down it pushes up the pivoted intermediate lever. The movement of this lever does three things:*

*1 It lifts the damper off the string by means of the vertical rod.*

*2 It throws the hammer against the string by means of the hopper which engages in the notch of the hammer butt.*

*3 It brings the hammer check closer to the hammer, ready to receive the hammer when it rebounds.*

*The tape, which is attached to the hammer butt at one end and to a wire post at the other, is pulled tight by the hammer's movement and so speeds the hammer's return.*

*The hammer has been pulled back and rests against the hammer check. When the key is released, the hopper will slip back into the notch in the hammer butt, ready for another blow.*

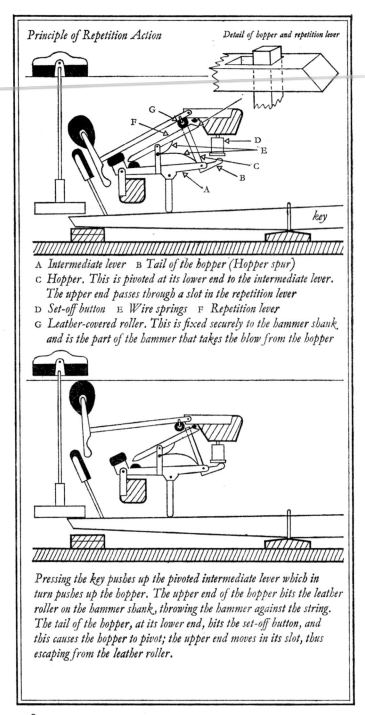

*Principle of Repetition Action*

*Detail of hopper and repetition lever*

A *Intermediate lever* B *Tail of the hopper (Hopper spur)*
C *Hopper. This is pivoted at its lower end to the intermediate lever.*
   *The upper end passes through a slot in the repetition lever*
D *Set-off button* E *Wire springs* F *Repetition lever*
G *Leather-covered roller. This is fixed securely to the hammer shank*
   *and is the part of the hammer that takes the blow from the hopper*

*Pressing the key pushes up the pivoted intermediate lever which in
turn pushes up the hopper. The upper end of the hopper hits the leather
roller on the hammer shank, throwing the hammer against the string.
The tail of the hopper, at its lower end, hits the set-off button, and
this causes the hopper to pivot; the upper end moves in its slot, thus
escaping from the leather roller.*

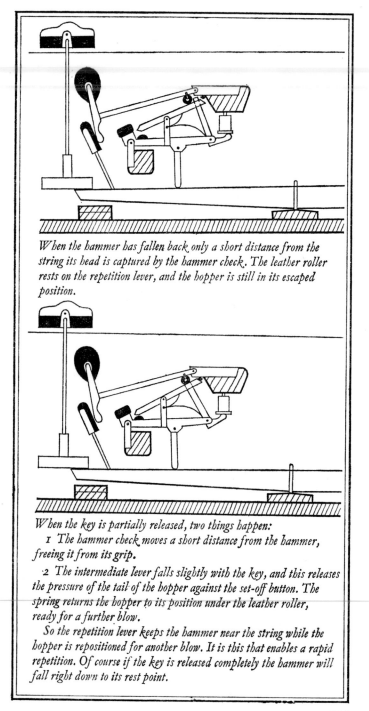

When the hammer has fallen back only a short distance from the string its head is captured by the hammer check. The leather roller rests on the repetition lever, and the hopper is still in its escaped position.

When the key is partially released, two things happen:

   *1* The hammer check moves a short distance from the hammer, freeing it from its grip.

   *2* The intermediate lever falls slightly with the key, and this releases the pressure of the tail of the hopper against the set-off button. The spring returns the hopper to its position under the leather roller, ready for a further blow.

So the repetition lever keeps the hammer near the string while the hopper is repositioned for another blow. It is this that enables a rapid repetition. Of course if the key is released completely the hammer will fall right down to its rest point.